AUSTRALIA REMEMBERS 6

Wartime Nurses

Care and Compassion

BIG SKY PUBLISHING

www.bigskypublishing.com.au

JACQUI HALPIN

We acknowledge the traditional owners of country throughout Australia and recognise their continuing connection to land, waters and culture. We pay our respects to their Elders past, present and emerging.

Aboriginal and Torres Strait Islander readers are advised that this book contains images of people who have passed away.

First published 2022

Big Sky Publishing Pty Ltd
PO Box 303, Newport, NSW 2106, Australia
Phone: 1300 364 611
Email: info@bigskypublishing.com.au
Web: www.bigskypublishing.com.au

Cover Design and Typesetting: Think Productions
Editing by Allison Marlow Paterson and Catherine McCullagh

A catalogue record for this book is available from the National Library of Australia

National Library of Australia Cataloguing-in-Publication entry
Author: Jacqui Halpin
Title: Australia Remembers 6: Wartime Nurses: Care and Compassion
978-1-922615-59-6 (HB)
978-1-922615-60-2 (PB)

Front cover images:
Left to right: Modern-day ADF red cross brassard (courtesy Department of Defence); Matron Ida Greaves, seated centre, and nursing sisters of The Australian Voluntary Hospital, August 1914 (courtesy Newcastle Museum); WWI AANS sleeve badge (courtesy The Queensland Women's Historical Association, Miegunyah House Museum).

Dedication

For my mother, Sister Betty Rumney,
an exceptional nurse and an even better mother.

CONTENTS

Chapter 1

A HISTORY OF CARING

Royal Australian Army Nursing Corps (RAANC) emblem.

For over 100 years, Australia's military nurses have risked their lives to save others. In their caring, capable hands, sick and wounded soldiers found comfort, healing and hope.

What is a Nurse?

A nurse is a person trained to care for the sick, wounded or injured. There is no greater need for such trained personnel than in times of war.

Pro Humanitate is Latin and means 'For Humanity'. Why do you think the Royal Australian Army Nursing Corps chose this as its motto?

While the colonial governments were reluctant to send women into a war zone, the New South Wales Army Nursing Service **Reserve** (NSWANSR) was formed in May 1899 as part of the New South Wales Army Medical Corps. Matron Ellen Julia 'Nellie' Gould was asked to be Lady Superintendent. She and her 24 nurses formed the first Australian military nursing organisation.

FAST FACT!

A nursing sister is a qualified or registered nurse. The term 'sister' is carried over from many years ago when caring for the sick was mostly the job of nuns from religious orders who were called 'sisters'. The Matron was the sister in charge of the nursing and the nurses at a hospital.

DID YOU KNOW?

It was British nurse Florence Nightingale who first showed military leaders how important quality nursing care was to the survival and recovery of wounded and sick soldiers. Her improvements in cleanliness, nutrition and the general care of her patients during the Crimean War (1853–1856) decreased the death rate at the military hospital she managed by two-thirds.

Florence Nightingale carried a lamp and walked the wards at night to give aid and comfort to her patients. She became known as 'the Lady with the Lamp' and the founder of modern nursing (Portrait courtesy of the Russell Family, Jimbour Station).

NSWANSR nurses sent to South Africa. Matron Nellie Gould is in the middle row, third from the left (courtesy RAANC archives).

FAST FACT!

More than 60 nurses from across the Australian colonies served in South Africa during the Boer War (1899-1902). Some even paid their own way or were supported by family, friends or sponsors.

'... 300 patients, nearly all typhoid and dysentery. The poor fellows seem to have no strength left ... it takes one all her time in trying to save them. How dreadful these diseases have been.'

Sister Bessie Pocock, NSWANSR, The Australian National Boer War Memorial website

When the **Boer War** broke out between Great Britain and the **Boers** in South Africa in October 1899, Australia was not yet united as a nation. The six separate colonies sent troops to fight for Great Britain. In total, over 16,000 men volunteered. Nurses also volunteered to care for these troops.

When Matron Nellie Gould and 13 nursing sisters from the NSWANSR set sail for South Africa in January 1900, they became the first group of Australian military nurses to be sent to war.

FAST FACT!

Typhoid is a disease caused by a bacteria which produces high fever, diarrhoea and dehydration. It is spread by eating or drinking contaminated food or water.

Sister Bessie Pocock, third from the left, with hospital staff and patients (courtesy RAANC archives).

FAST FACT!

More soldiers died from typhoid during the Boer War than from war wounds.

Their training in **civilian** hospitals did little to prepare Nellie and her nurses for the dreadful conditions in the Australian and British military hospitals to which they were sent. They spent many hours scrubbing floors and cleaning. Apart from the filthy conditions, there was often a lack of food and equipment. A typhoid epidemic caused by contaminated water made their job even harder. In fact, the nurses spent more time treating sick soldiers than wounded ones.

Matron Nellie Gould

Matron Nellie Gould returned to Sydney after the Boer War and worked for the education and welfare of nurses. When World War I broke out, she enlisted in the Australian Army Nursing Service. Despite being 54 years old (over the age limit to enlist), she was accepted and appointed Matron of the 2nd Australian General Hospital. She served in Egypt, then France and England. Nellie was awarded the Royal Red Cross in 1916 for her service to nursing.

FAST FACT!

Sister Frances Emma 'Fanny' Hines from Victoria was the first Australian military nurse to die on active service. She died of pneumonia while caring for sick soldiers during the Boer War. Sister Fanny Hines was buried with full military honours.

Victorian nurses who went to South Africa in March 1900. Front row, left to right: Sisters Fanny Hines, Julia Anderson, Marianne Rawson, Ellen Walter and Annie Thomson (courtesy AWM P04544.003).

Australian nurses were highly praised for their hard work and resourcefulness. Three were awarded Royal Red Cross Medals.

With nurses now caring for them instead of only doctors and **medical orderlies**, many more soldiers recovered from their wounds and illnesses. By the end of the Boer War in 1902, the Australian authorities recognised that military hospitals needed nurses. The Australian Army Nursing Service Reserve was established in 1903 to provide trained nurses to serve in military hospitals.

Medical Breakthrough

The X-ray machine was invented by Wilhelm Roentgen in 1895. During the Boer War X-ray machines were used in several military hospitals.

How would having X-ray machines in military hospitals help with the treatment of wounded soldiers?

Chapter 2

WORLD WAR I – SETTING UP HOSPITALS IN TENTS AND PALACES

World War I erupted on 4 August 1914 when Germany invaded Belgium, prompting Britain to declare war on Germany. Thousands of Australian men volunteered to fight as part of the British Empire and the Australian **Imperial** Force (AIF) was established. The Australian Army Medical Corps (AAMC) provided hospitals, doctors and nurses as part of the AIF.

An important part of the AAMC was the newly formed Australian Army Nursing Service (AANS). It was made up of nurses from the Australian Army Nursing Service Reserve and other nurses who enlisted.

Some nurses joined up as a way to be closer to male relatives who were serving overseas. Some joined for the adventure or the chance to advance their careers. But many joined as an act of **patriotism**. They knew nurses would be badly needed and wanted to care for 'our boys'.

AANS nurses departing Melbourne in May 1916 (courtesy AWM PB 0381).

DID YOU KNOW?

Over 3,000 Australian nurses served overseas during World War I. Most joined the AANS, but many others served in British hospitals. Others joined aid organisations such as the Red Cross and St John's Ambulance Brigade, or volunteered to work in privately run hospitals in France, England and other parts of Europe.

AANS Sleeve Badge (courtesy The Queensland Women's Historical Association, Miegunyah House Museum).

Enlistment Requirements

To enlist in the AANS, nurses needed to be aged between 25 and 40, single or widowed and have had at least three years' training in a general hospital. Like soldiers, nurses had to pass a medical examination to prove they were fit and healthy.

Why do you think it was important for nurses to be fit and in good health?

How do you think modern-day nurses would feel about not being able to serve as a nurse if they were married?

...you don't know how glad I am and thankful that I took the notion into my head to take on nursing. I have never regretted that, for it has opened up opportunities that I would not have had and that I would not have missed for anything.

Sister Jessie Tomlins who served in Egypt with the AANS, Australian War Memorial website

In November 1914, Australian nurses once again set sail for war, this time aboard the first convoy of troopships to leave Australia.

During the long sea voyage, the nurses assisted the medical officers (doctors) to vaccinate the soldiers against **smallpox** and typhoid. They also trained men to work as medical orderlies.

A nurse teaches trainee medical orderlies how to apply bandages on board *Mooltan* in 1915 (courtesy Mitchell Library, State Library of New South Wales. ML PXE 698 AW Savage).

Medical Breakthrough

Developed in 1896 by Almroth Wright, the typhoid vaccine was compulsory for AIF soldiers and nurses during World War I and saved thousands of lives.

The 1st Australian General Hospital (1 AGH), and the 2nd Australian General Hospital (2 AGH) were the two largest Australian military hospitals in Egypt. 1 AGH occupied the magnificent Heliopolis Palace Hotel outside Cairo. The nurses worked hard turning the grand dining halls and guest rooms into wards. The King of Belgium's suite became an operating theatre. 2 AGH took over Mena House, a former royal hunting lodge close to the pyramids at Giza.

DID YOU KNOW?

During the war many buildings in Egypt, the Middle East, India, Europe, England and even in Australia were taken over by the War Office for use as hospitals, casualty clearing stations and convalescent homes.

The Heliopolis Palace Hotel was taken over by the War Office to use as a hospital (courtesy Museums Victoria Collections 107441). Can you see the tent wards in the hotel grounds?

DID YOU KNOW?

There were no hospitals or nurses at Gallipoli. At the beginning of the Gallipoli campaign, the nearest hospitals were based in Egypt, which was a three and a half day journey by sea. Australian, British, Canadian and Indian military hospitals were later established on the Greek Island of Lemnos which was much closer to the fighting and could be reached by ship in four hours.

Nurses, hospital staff and wounded soldiers, Mena House, 2 AGH, Egypt, 1915 (courtesy Mitchell Library, State Library of New South Wales).

FAST FACT!

ANZAC stands for Australian and New Zealand Army Corps, a combined force which fought with British and French soldiers against Turkish troops on the Gallipoli Peninsula in Turkey during World War I.

The former skating rink of Cairo's Luna Park filled with casualties from Gallipoli, 1 AGH, 1915. Can you find the nurses amongst all the patients? (courtesy AWM P01350.013).

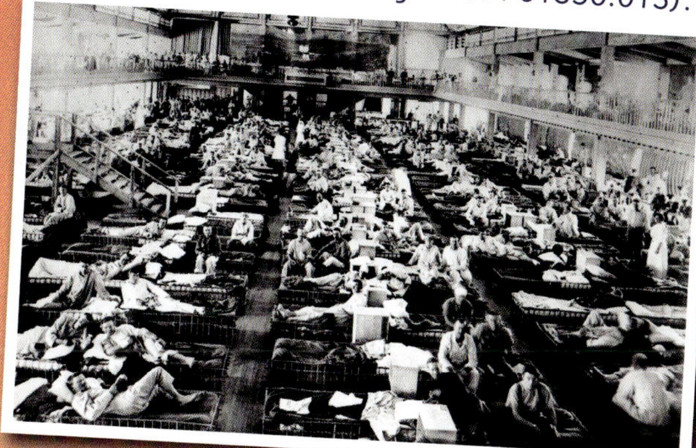

Nurses with their patients on the merry-go-round ward at 1 AGH, Luna Park, Cairo, 1915 (courtesy Museums Victoria Collections 107482).

Do you think it would have been more difficult to care for patients in a ward set up on a merry-go-round?

On 25 April 1915, ANZAC troops landed on the beach at Gallipoli. A few days later the Australian wounded from Gallipoli began arriving at the hospitals in Cairo. Brought by hospital trains and ambulances from the ships, they came pouring in by the hundreds. 1 AGH soon increased from 500 beds to 2,500 and spread into nearby buildings, including an aerodrome and an amusement park.

2 AGH took over the Ghezireh Palace where Matron Nellie Gould and her team of nurses set up an extra 1,500 beds. The nurses worked around the clock **dressing** battle wounds, washing, feeding and caring for their many patients.

DID YOU KNOW?

A field ambulance is not a type of vehicle but a military unit. The field ambulance included medical officers, stretcher-bearers, ambulance drivers, dentists, even soldiers in charge of sanitation. These units had the vital role of giving first aid and transporting sick or wounded soldiers to advanced dressing stations, casualty clearing stations or hospitals. Vehicles used for transporting casualties could be anything from hand carts to motorbikes, ships, bicycles, horse-drawn carts, cars, trucks, vans, donkeys, even camels!

With the hospitals in Egypt overcrowded, more beds were urgently needed. The Greek Island of Lemnos was chosen as the site for the 3rd Australian General Hospital (3 AGH) under Matron Grace Wilson.

When Grace and her 80 nurses arrived on the barren island of Lemnos in August 1915, they found 150 wounded soldiers lying on the ground. The tents and other hospital supplies had been sent to the wrong place and would not arrive on Lemnos for almost three weeks.

The nurses used whatever they could find to treat the wounded. They tore up some of their own clothes to make bandages and used their own crockery and cutlery for their patients. Water was scarce. Nurses washed their patients using seawater and their own soap.

FAST FACT!

The Rising Sun Badge is the official badge of the Australian Army. A bronze Rising Sun Badge is traditionally worn on the upturned side brim of Australian soldiers' slouch hats. AANS nurses, as members of the AIF, wore a silver Rising Sun Badge as part of their uniform.

Ward Uniform

The AANS ward uniform in World War I was an ankle-length dress in grey cotton with long sleeves and a detachable white collar and cuffs. A long, starched, white apron with a bib front was worn over the dress and a scarlet shoulder cape, fastened at the throat with a silver Rising Sun Badge. The uniform was worn with black stockings and shoes and a white linen veil one yard (91.5cm) square.

DID YOU KNOW?

The nurses' short red ward cape was known as a 'tippet'.

This AANS silver Rising Sun Badge belonged to Sister Constance Keys (courtesy John Oxley Library, State Library of Queensland).

Matron Grace Wilson ~ A Woman of Understanding

A few days before Matron Grace Wilson landed on Lemnos, she learned that her beloved brother had been killed at Anzac Cove. Despite this dreadful news, Grace carried on with the enormous task of treating the sick and wounded from Gallipoli.

Grace remained in charge of 3 AGH when it was transferred to Egypt, England and then France. She was awarded the Royal Red Cross 1st Class for her outstanding service in wartime and was later awarded the Florence Nightingale Medal. Grace left the AANS in 1920 but was made **Matron-in-Chief** of the Australian Army Nursing Service Reserve in 1925. At the age of 60, she was called up for full-time duty in World War II.

> *At times I think we could not have carried on without her. She was not only a capable Matron, but what is more, a woman of understanding.*
>
> Sister Nita Selwyn-Smith, 3 AGH, referring to Matron Grace Wilson, *Willingly into the Fray*, Catherine McCullagh, page 35

Matron Grace Wilson doing her rounds on Lemnos (courtesy AWM A05332).

FAST FACT

The Australian hospitals did not only care for Australian and New Zealand troops. They nursed French, British and other Allied soldiers, as well as caring for Turkish and German prisoners of war.

How would you feel about caring for an enemy patient?

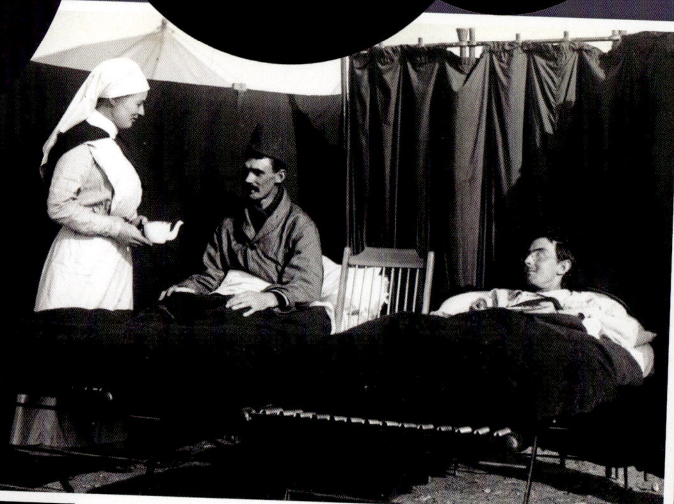

A Turkish prisoner of war being treated by an Australian nurse at 3 AGH, Lemnos, in 1915 (courtesy Mitchell Library, State Library of New South Wales).

Nurses with their patients in a tent ward on Lemnos in 1915 (courtesy Mitchell Library, State Library of New South Wales). Did you notice that the floor is a tarpaulin?

DID YOU KNOW?

The donkeys used to transport the wounded on Gallipoli, including the famous Simpson's donkey, came from the island of Lemnos.

FAST FACT!

Australian involvement in the Gallipoli campaign lasted from 25 April to 20 December 1915. In that short period of time, 8,709 AIF soldiers were killed and 19,441 wounded.

What difficulties do you think there would be in caring for wounded and sick patients in tents?

The tent wards of 3 AGH on the island of Lemnos (courtesy State Library of New South Wales, FL1523996).

Nurses sometimes fell ill with the same diseases as their patients. These sick nurses are being cared for by their fellow sisters (courtesy Mitchell Library, State Library of New South Wales).

Chapter 3

HOSPITAL SHIPS – SERVING AT SEA

Many Australian nurses served on British and Australian hospital ships during World War I. These ships were often converted passenger liners and were used as floating hospitals. Hospital ships were protected from enemy attack by the Geneva Conventions. To make hospital ships easily recognisable, their hulls were painted white, with a wide horizontal green band and big red crosses. Despite this, many hospital ships were attacked and sunk during the war.

Under the Geneva Conventions, strict rules applied to hospital ships. They were only to be used to transport sick and wounded patients and not for the movement of troops or equipment.

Nurses on board the hospital ship *Karoola* practise lifeboat drill (courtesy AWM P02626.002).

FAST FACT!

The Geneva Conventions are a set of international rules that cover the treatment of those wounded on the battlefield, civilians and prisoners of war. They were first developed in Geneva, Switzerland, in 1864.

? Why do you think it was important for nurses to have life jackets and know how to use lifeboats?

FAST FACT!

The only Australian nurse to die as a result of enemy action during World War I was Sister Edith Blake. Edith was serving with the British forces and was on board the hospital ship *Glenart Castle* on her way to pick up wounded from France. The ship was fully lit and clearly marked as a hospital ship when it was sunk by a German torpedo. Most of the staff and crew lost their lives, including all eight nurses on board.

Hospital ships carried wounded and sick soldiers from Gallipoli to the hospitals in Egypt, and the islands of Lemnos, Imbros and Malta. They were also used to transport seriously wounded soldiers to England for treatment. Many badly wounded Australian soldiers who were permanently 'unfit for duty' were brought home to Australia on hospital ships.

Nursing at Sea

Nursing on hospital ships was difficult because of the cramped conditions. Fresh water and other medical supplies were often rationed. Operating on patients, giving medication and dressing wounds in rough seas were a huge challenge. Nurses sometimes needed to strap their patients into their beds during bad weather.

Australian hospital ship *Kanowna* leaving Alexandria, Egypt, 1916 (courtesy AWM C01054).

Wounded soldiers waiting to be hoisted aboard a hospital ship anchored off Anzac Cove, 1915 (courtesy AWM A02740).

Sick and wounded soldiers from Gallipoli were ferried out to the hospital ships on smaller boats which were often fired on by the enemy. Nurses on the ships were also in danger of being hit by stray bullets.

Nurses on board the hospital ship HMHS *Assaye*, 1915. Matron Bessie Pocock is holding the ship's cat (courtesy State Library of South Australia).

There were not enough hospital ships to cope with the enormous number of wounded men from Gallipoli. So transport ships were also used to carry the sick and wounded. These ships were not protected from enemy attack and there were no nurses on board to care for the wounded men. As a result, many died on the way to hospital.

Medical Breakthrough

The use of tetanus anti-serum, taken from horses infected with a modified tetanus toxin, saved many lives during World War I. Wounded soldiers were injected with the serum to prevent them developing tetanus. Tetanus was contracted when wounds became contaminated with dirt containing the tetanus bacteria.

Chapter 4

THE WESTERN FRONT – NURSES UNDER FIRE

Most of the fighting during World War I occurred on the Western Front, a series of trenches and fortifications that ran for over 700 kilometres across Belgium and France as far south as the Swiss border. Approximately 295,000 Australian soldiers served on the Western Front. Some 45,000 were killed and more than 130,000 were wounded.

Australian nurses served in France and Belgium in Australian and Allied hospitals and casualty clearing stations. They cared for Allied troops and also German prisoners of war. Nurses worked long hours and those close to the front line were often at risk of enemy attack.

Tent wards covered in snow in France. Nurses had a difficult time trying to keep themselves and their patients warm in winter. Often it was so cold that medicines froze in their bottles (courtesy AWM P00156.072).

Medical Breakthrough

The discovery during World War I of a chemical (sodium citrate) that stopped blood from clotting meant that blood collected from donors could be stored on ice for up to four weeks and used where and when it was needed. By 1918 blood transfusions were being used extensively on the Western Front to treat wounded soldiers, saving countless lives.

DID YOU KNOW?

Nurses also squeezed in time to write letters for their patients who were too sick to write and often wrote sympathy letters to the families of their patients who had died.

Why do you think blood transfusions were so necessary during the war?

FAST FACT

Nurses were not permitted to wear make-up, perfume or jewellery, except for a watch.

Nissen hut wards of 1 AGH, Rouen, France, September 1918. Can you see the walls made of sandbags? These were to help protect the buildings and their occupants from aerial bombings (courtesy AWM E03423).

Tent wards of 1 AGH, Rouen, France, September 1918 (courtesy AWM E03447K).

Nurses assigned to casualty clearing stations had one of the most difficult and dangerous jobs. These stations were based as close to the fighting as possible so that they could quickly treat wounded men. They were often just tents or huts and were under constant threat of enemy bullets, bombings or being overrun by advancing enemy forces. They needed to be ready to pack up and move quickly as the **front line** advanced or retreated. Nurses were often on duty 16 hours a day for weeks on end without a break.

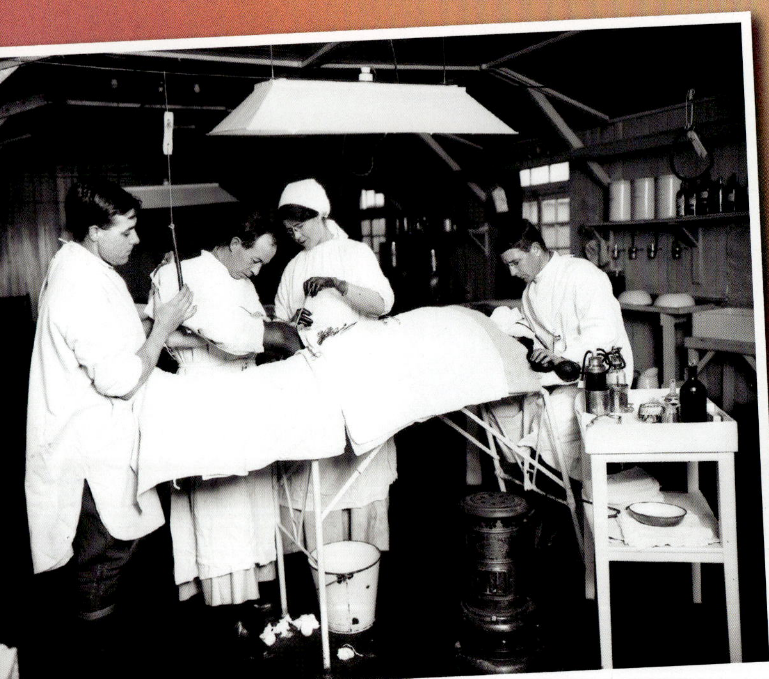

An operating theatre, France 1917 (courtesy AWM E01304).

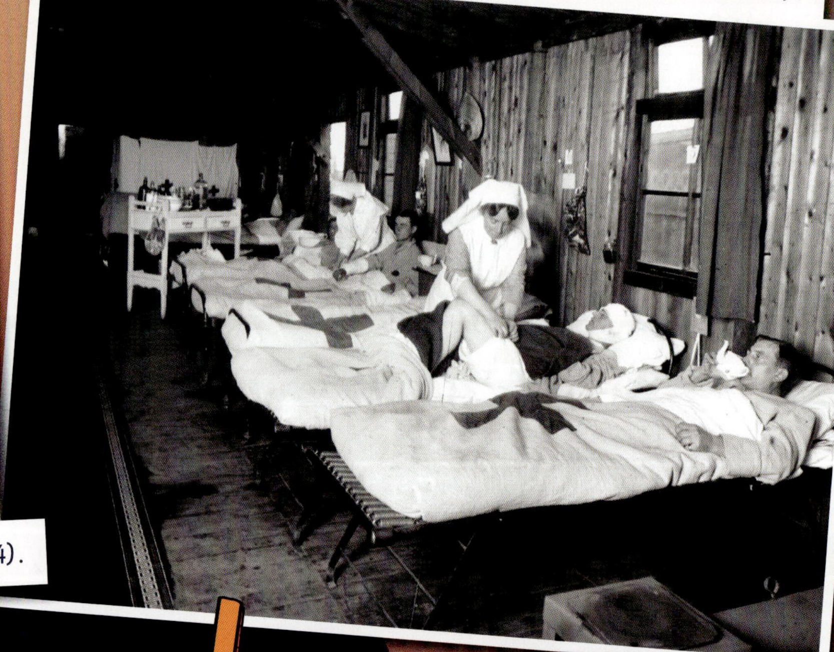

Nurses tending to their patients in 1917 (courtesy AWM E04623).

FAST FACT!

With only their red cross armbands for protection, stretcher-bearers collected and carried the wounded from the battlefield to aid posts. These brave men were equipped with just their first aid bags and performed their duty in all conditions, even under heavy enemy fire.

AANS nurse, Sister Queenie Avenell, with some of her patients at an Australian military hospital in England, 1917 (courtesy Pat Richardson).

FAST FACT !

Five hundred Australian nurses served in hospitals in India during World War I. Another 380 served on the Salonika front in Greece.

AANS nurse and some of her patients in Salonika (also known as Thessalonika), Greece (courtesy AWM H03708).

?

Do you see the mosquito nets above each bed? Why do you think mosquito nets were important?

Chapter 5

DETERMINED TO SERVE – VOLUNTEER NURSES

Apart from the many nurses serving with the AANS and with the British Army, hundreds of Australian nurses volunteered to work in privately funded hospitals during World War I. The first Australian hospital established in France was the Australian Voluntary Hospital. Organised by Lady Dudley, the ex-wife of the former Governor-General of Australia, it was opened in August 1914. It was staffed by Australian doctors (men only) and nurses who were already living in the United Kingdom at the outbreak of war.

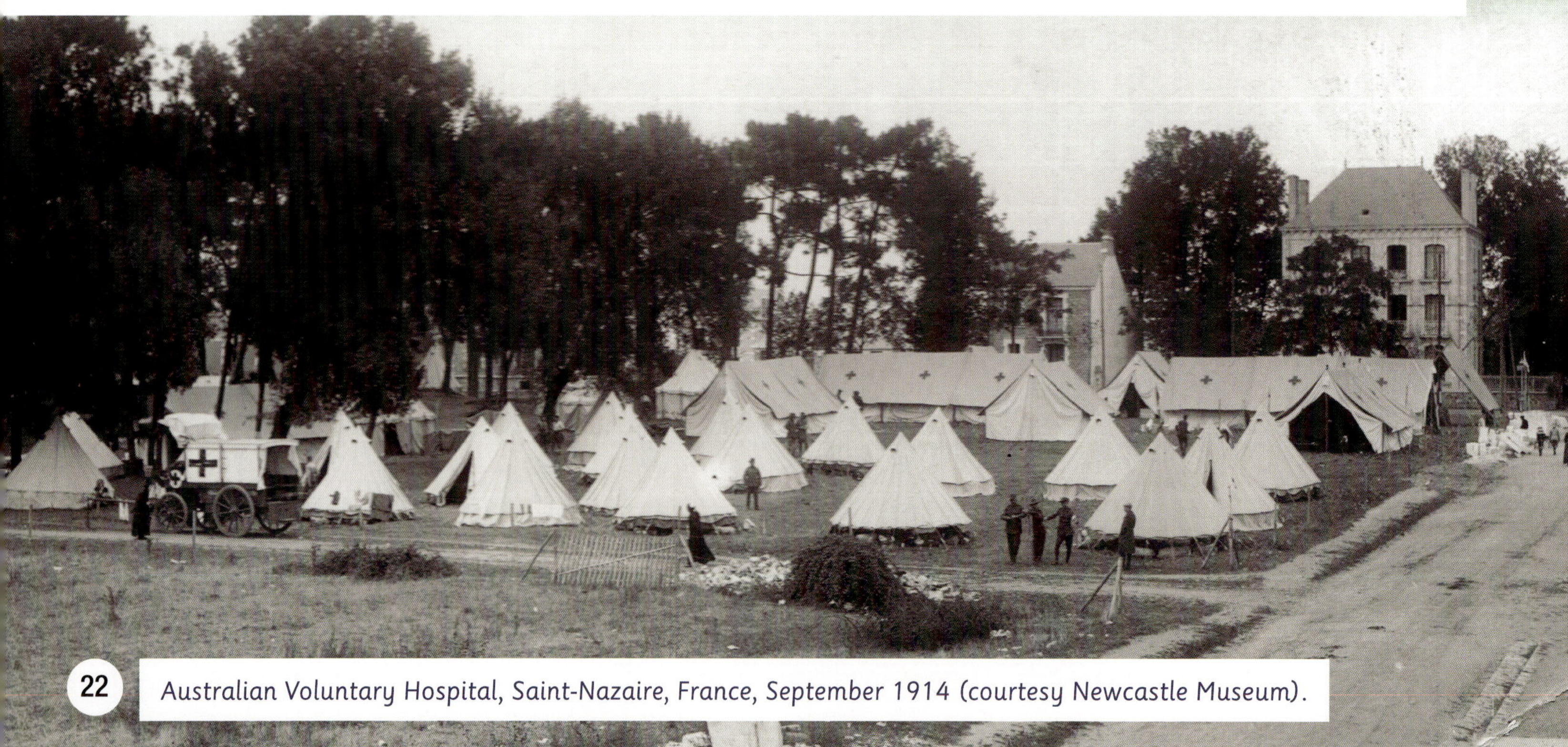

Australian Voluntary Hospital, Saint-Nazaire, France, September 1914 (courtesy Newcastle Museum).

The Bluebirds ~ A Gift for France

The Bluebirds was a group of 20 civilian nurses and one masseuse who were recruited by the Australian Red Cross as a gift for France which was in desperate need of nurses during World War I. They were sponsored by the Australian Jockey Club and their uniforms were made by David Jones department stores. They were called 'The Bluebirds' because of their navy-blue uniforms. These courageous Australian nurses operated under the same dangerous and harrowing conditions as AANS nurses but received no military medals from the Australian or British governments, no war pensions, and some had to pay their own way home to Australia after the war.

The Bluebirds and their French language teacher waiting to board the hospital ship *Kanowna*, Melbourne, July 1916 (courtesy AWM PB0483).

Why do you think it was important for The Bluebirds to know how to speak French?

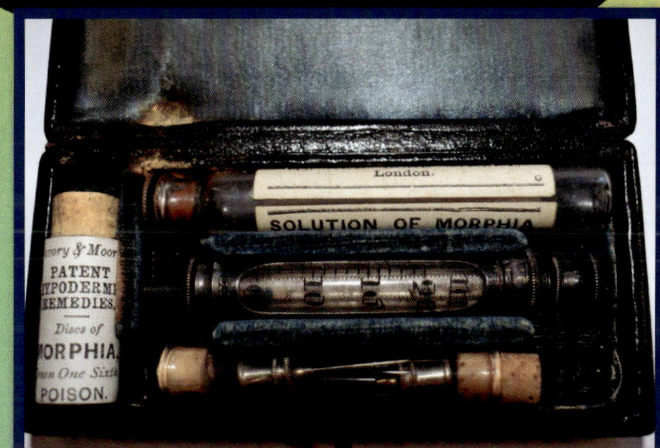

A glass syringe and morphine ampoule similar to the ones used during World War I (courtesy Museum of Nursing History, Royal Brisbane and Women's Hospital).

Nurse Anaesthetists

A shortage of doctors in the desperately busy operating theatres of casualty clearing stations meant some nurses were able to increase their skills in ways not possible in civilian hospitals in Australia. They used scalpels to remove bullets, chose when to give morphine to patients in pain, and some were even trained to give anaesthetics.

DID YOU KNOW?

Before the introduction of anaesthetics in the 1840s, surgery was performed with little or no pain relief. Patients were awake throughout the operation causing great suffering and distress.

Australian nurses Claire Trestrail, Caroline Wilson and Catherine Tully were working in a privately funded hospital set up in a disused concert hall in Antwerp, Belgium, when the Germans bombed the city in October 1914. These brave nurses sheltered their patients in the cellars. As the German Army closed in, they stayed to make sure their patients were safely evacuated. Then they fled the burning town perched on top of a double-decker bus, crossing the only bridge out of the city just before it was blown up.

Sister Claire Trestrail (seated) with a ward assistant and patients at the Auxiliary Hospital Unit in Belgium (courtesy AWM P08673.002).

Survivor

South Australian nurse Sister Caroline Wilson, who survived the destruction and invasion of Antwerp, had previously survived almost being washed overboard when the ship on which she was travelling to England was struck by a tidal wave. On 15 July 1918 she was among the survivors of HMAT *Barunga* when it was torpedoed and sunk.

The Red Cross

A red cross on a white background is an internationally recognised symbol that means 'Don't Shoot! We are not part of the fight'. The symbol was chosen over 150 years ago by the Red Cross Society because it is the reverse of the Swiss flag and the founder was Swiss. It is used to protect medical teams, their patients, equipment, buildings and vehicles in times of war and conflict.

A World War I Red Cross Armband (courtesy AWM REL31246).

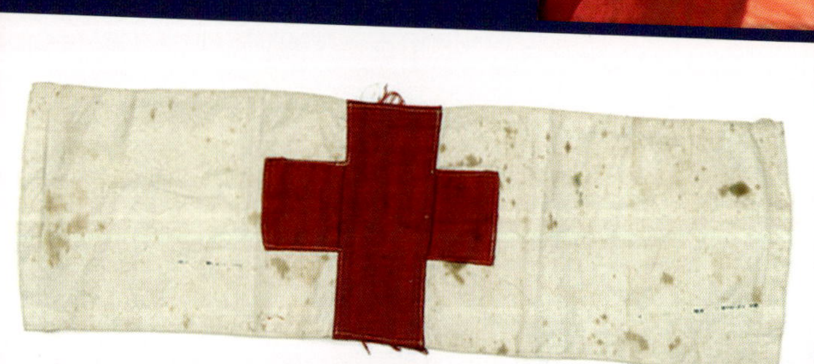

VADs, known as Red Cross nurses, with some of their Australian patients during World War I (courtesy John Oxley Library, State Library of Queensland).

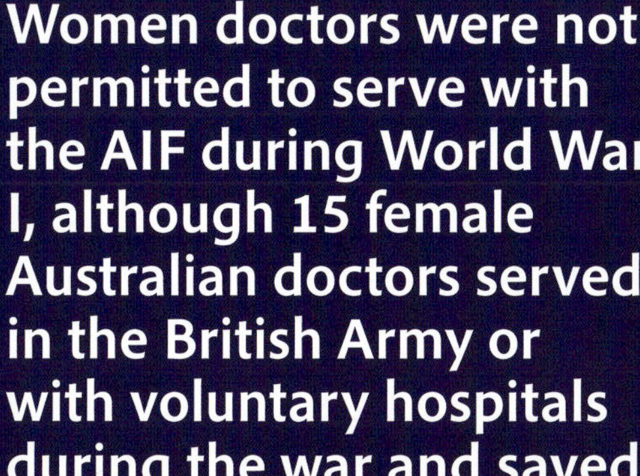

DID YOU KNOW?

Women doctors were not permitted to serve with the AIF during World War I, although 15 female Australian doctors served in the British Army or with voluntary hospitals during the war and saved thousands of lives.

Voluntary Aid Detachment (VAD)

Hundreds of Australian women worked in Voluntary Aid Detachments (VADs) during World War I. Established by the Australian Red Cross and the Order of St John at the start of the war, VADs served in military and Red Cross hospitals, on trains, and in convalescent homes in Australia and overseas. They worked as assistant nurses, ward maids and orderlies. VADs had training in first aid, basic patient care and cooking for the sick, but were not trained nurses. They wore a large red cross on the front of their uniforms.

Chapter 6

DANGEROUS WATERS AND DREADED DISEASES

During World War I some 155,000 Australians were wounded on overseas service. Wounded or sick Australian soldiers who would not recover enough to be sent back to the front within six months were returned to Australia. Many of these soldiers were evacuated on British and Australian transport ships. AANS nurses were assigned to these ships to care for the wounded and sick on board.

Medical Breakthrough

The invention of the Thomas splint, which was used to immobilise the legs of soldiers with fractured femurs (broken thigh bones), saved thousands of lives during World War I. The Thomas splint is still used today.

Nurses wearing lifebelts on board an army transport ship, 1916 (courtesy John Oxley Library, State Library of Queensland).

Sister Elizabeth Kenny, who became famous worldwide for her revolutionary treatment for the crippling disease of polio (poliomyelitis), served on transport ships during WWI. She claimed to have perfected her treatment of massage and muscle strengthening whilst treating recovering soldiers on board these ships (courtesy John Oxley Library, State Library of Queensland).

DID YOU KNOW?

A number of masseuses (later called physiotherapists) served during World War I. They worked in hospitals in Egypt, France, Britain and Australia, and on hospital ships and sea transports.

FAST FACT!

Twenty-five Australian nurses died on active service during World War I. All but one died from illnesses or infections contracted while caring for their soldier patients. Four more died shortly after the war as a result of diseases they picked up while serving.

HMAT *Themistocles* returns to Australia loaded with troops, 1917 (courtesy State Library Victoria, Barnes J E, photographer).

When World War I ended in November 1918, another even more deadly war began — the fight against the Spanish Flu pandemic. This strain of influenza began to affect troops in the trenches early in 1918. It spread rapidly among the returning soldiers on troopships causing hundreds of deaths. By the end of 1918 it had reached Australia. Quarantine stations, isolation wards and influenza hospitals were quickly set up across the country to treat the infected. By the time the pandemic was over, in December 1919, almost 40% of the Australian population had been infected and over 12,000 had died. The Spanish Flu was the deadliest flu outbreak in history. It killed at least 50 million people worldwide, almost three times the total number of people killed during World War I.

AANS nurses at the Quarantine Camp on Jubilee Oval, South Australia, in 1919. The nurse in the front row far right is Sister Caroline Wilson. Having survived tidal waves, bombings and a sinking ship, she went on to nurse victims of the Spanish Flu and survived that as well, living to be 95 (courtesy State Library of South Australia, PRG 1638/2/53).

FAST FACT!

Five AANS nurses and one civilian nurse who volunteered to care for infected soldiers at Quarantine Stations died from Spanish Flu.

Do you see any comparisons between the Spanish Flu pandemic and the COVID-19 pandemic?

DID YOU KNOW?

In an effort to stop the spread of Spanish Flu, state borders in Australia were closed. Wearing masks was made compulsory in some places, and people who did not comply could be arrested. Australians were advised to avoid crowds, and cinemas and schools were closed. Some schools introduced lessons by correspondence.

DID YOU KNOW?

The Australian Red Cross supplied over 700,000 face masks to the public during the Spanish Flu pandemic. VADs volunteered to work in hospitals and quarantine stations. Five VADs died from Spanish Flu while caring for patients.

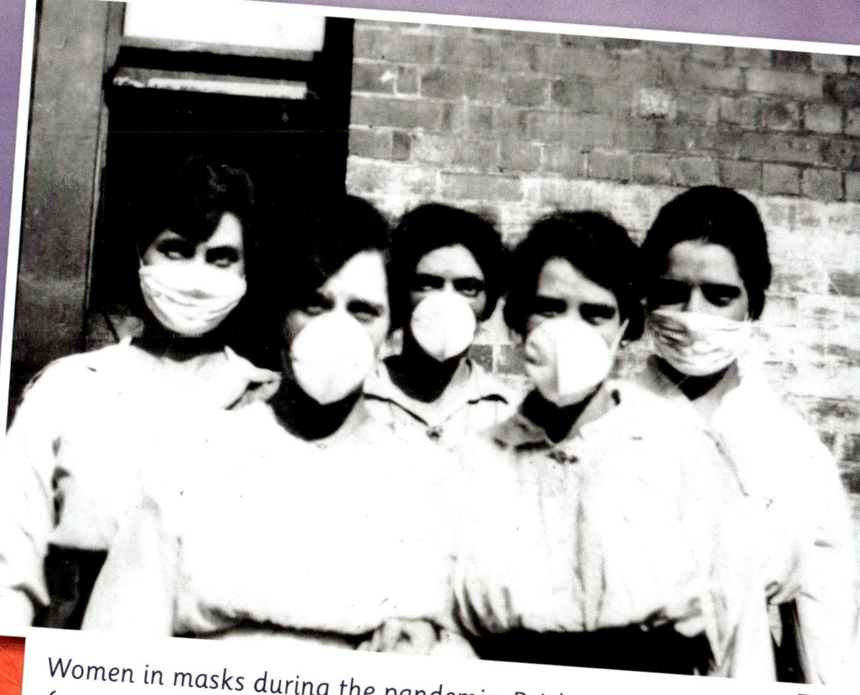

Women in masks during the pandemic, Brisbane, 1919 (courtesy John Oxley Library, State Library of Queensland).

Chapter 7

WORLD WAR II NURSES – DEVOTION TO DUTY

In September 1939, Nazi Germany invaded Poland. Britain and France declared war on Germany, and Australia also found itself at war. With the entry of Germany's allies, Italy and Japan, into the war, it became a global conflict. A new Australian volunteer force was formed and named the 2nd Australian Imperial Force. Nurses once again volunteered to accompany these troops to war.

Over 4,000 trained nurses served during World War II, most with the AANS. Like the nurses who volunteered in World War I, many joined out of patriotism and a sense of duty. They wanted to 'do their bit'. Others wanted adventure. Whatever their reasons, they were badly needed, brave and strong.

Matron Annie Sage, front row sixth from the left, with nurses and physiotherapists ready to board their troopship at Port Melbourne, 1940 (*Herald & Weekly Times* photograph, courtesy State Library Victoria).

AANS nurses parade on deck in their life jackets during a lifeboat drill, 1941 (*Argus* Newspaper Collection of Photographs, courtesy State Library Victoria).

During World War II, AANS nurses served in hospitals, casualty clearing stations, convalescent homes and hospital trains in the Middle East, the Mediterranean, South East Asia and the Pacific, Ceylon (now Sri Lanka) and in Britain and Australia. They also served on hospital ships and sea transports. Most had no previous experience of military nursing.

The first group to leave comprised the nurses of the 2/1st AGH sent to the Middle East in January 1940. They were followed a few months later by the staff of the 2/2nd AGH under Matron Annie Sage. Conditions had not improved much since World War I. The nurses coped with equipment shortages and a lack of running water, lived and worked in tents, and battled dust storms and flies. They were sometimes housed in underground dugouts or abandoned hotels. They hid in slit trenches during enemy bombing raids and improvised ways to **sterilise** their instruments and equipment.

Nurses worked 12-hour shifts (often longer), six days a week for six weeks at a time before they were given any leave. When they ran out of beds, the nurses cared for their patients on stretchers on the floor.

The large red crosses painted on the roofs of hospital tents and huts did little to protect them. As enemy air raids became more and more frequent, blackouts were enforced and all lights needed to be covered or turned off.

Some of the nurses of the 2/1st AGH who had to cope with living and nursing in tents, Palestine, 1941 (courtesy Dulcie Thompson collection).

FAST FACT!

AANS nurses cared for Allied troops and enemy prisoners but, unlike in World War I, they mainly cared for sick and wounded Australian troops.

FAST FACT!

At the outbreak of war, the nurses enlisting in the AANS were still required to be either widowed or single. But this was changed in 1942 as more nurses were needed with the possibility of a Japanese invasion of Australia.

AANS nurses on board a troop train, Palestine (courtesy State Library Victoria).

Many World War II nurses worked close to the fighting. The nurses who were stationed in Tobruk in Libya, North Africa, helped evacuate 300 of their patients as German forces closed in. They begged to stay and care for their remaining patients but were ordered to evacuate only days before the port town was surrounded.

None of the courageous nurses serving under Matron Kathleen Best in Greece wanted to leave their patients as the German Army approached. When the order was given to evacuate, Matron Best had to choose who stayed. The rest were loaded onto trucks after dark and driven to the port of Navplion where they escaped by ship to the island of Crete. Matron Best and the remaining nurses were evacuated a few days later.

Australian and New Zealand nurses who escaped from Greece arrive on the island of Crete, 1941 (courtesy State Library Victoria).

DID YOU KNOW?

In March 1943, AANS nurses were given formal military officer ranks. Matrons were addressed as 'major', senior sisters as 'captain' and sisters as 'lieutenant'. Many nurses did not like being called by their army rank and preferred the traditional title, 'sister'.

I told the Sisters what was to happen and also made it clear to them that those who volunteered would stay behind with the hospital and that they would in all possibility be captured. I asked them to write on a slip of paper their names and either "stay" or "go" and hand them to me ... Not one Sister wrote "go" on her paper.

Matron Kathleen Best, 2/5th AGH, Greece, April 1941, *Guns and Brooches*, Jan Bassett, page 123

DID YOU KNOW?

In December 1942, the Australian Army Medical Women's Service (AAMWS) was formed, largely from VADs. Some 8,500 women worked within this service, in Australia and overseas, as assistants in nursing, radiology, pathology, laundry, clerical services and as orderlies. Without these dedicated women, army hospitals could not have coped with the immense number of wounded.

Members of the AAMWS returning to Australia after serving in military hospitals in the Middle East and Ceylon (Sri Lanka), 1943 (*Argus* Newspaper Collection of Photographs, courtesy State Library Victoria).

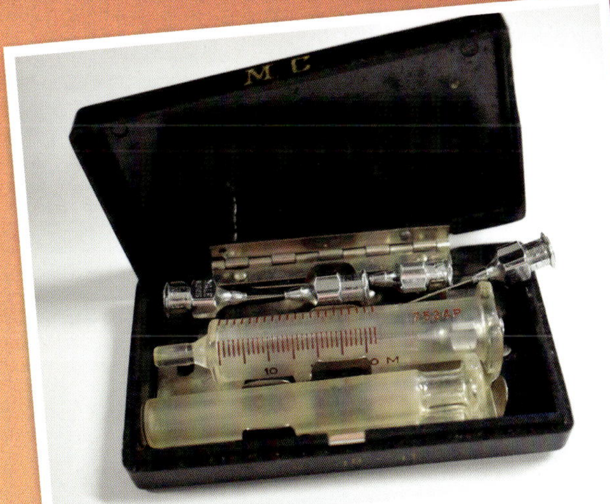

Reusable glass syringe and needles (courtesy Museum of Nursing History, Royal Brisbane and Women's Hospital).

DID YOU KNOW?

Prior to the 1950s, thermometers, syringes and intravenous therapy bottles were all made of glass. They were washed, sterilised and reused. Most equipment used by nurses in World War I and World War II was glass, ceramic or metal, and was not disposable.

Medical Breakthrough

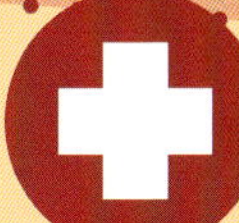

Penicillin was the first antibiotic. It was discovered in 1928 by Alexander Fleming. It was developed for use as a medical drug in 1938 by a team of British scientists led by Australian doctor Howard Florey. At the start of the war there was very little of this newly developed drug available but, by the end of the war, it was widely used. Penicillin saved the lives of thousands of soldiers who would normally have died from wound infections and diseases such as pneumonia. It is still one of the most widely used antibiotics in the world.

When Japan entered the war in December 1941, most Australian troops were withdrawn from the Middle East and sent to fight against the Japanese in the Pacific and New Guinea. AANS nurses were also recalled to serve in Australia, New Guinea and the Pacific.

The first AANS nurses arrived in New Guinea in April 1941 and were based in Rabaul, New Britain. From October 1942, additional AANS nurses and physiotherapists were stationed near Port Moresby to care for the wounded and sick from the Kokoda campaign. Later, other nurses served in Buna, Papua (now part of New Guinea) and various locations throughout the Pacific.

A nursing sister waters the tarpaulin floor of her tent ward at a Field Hospital in Port Moresby. Why do you think this would be necessary?

DID YOU KNOW?

Many military personnel suffered from malaria, an infectious, life-threatening disease carried by mosquitoes that causes fever, tiredness, vomiting and headaches. It is now preventable and curable.

Nurses on the island of Bougainville in 1945. Notice they are wearing their new uniform (courtesy AWM 078583).

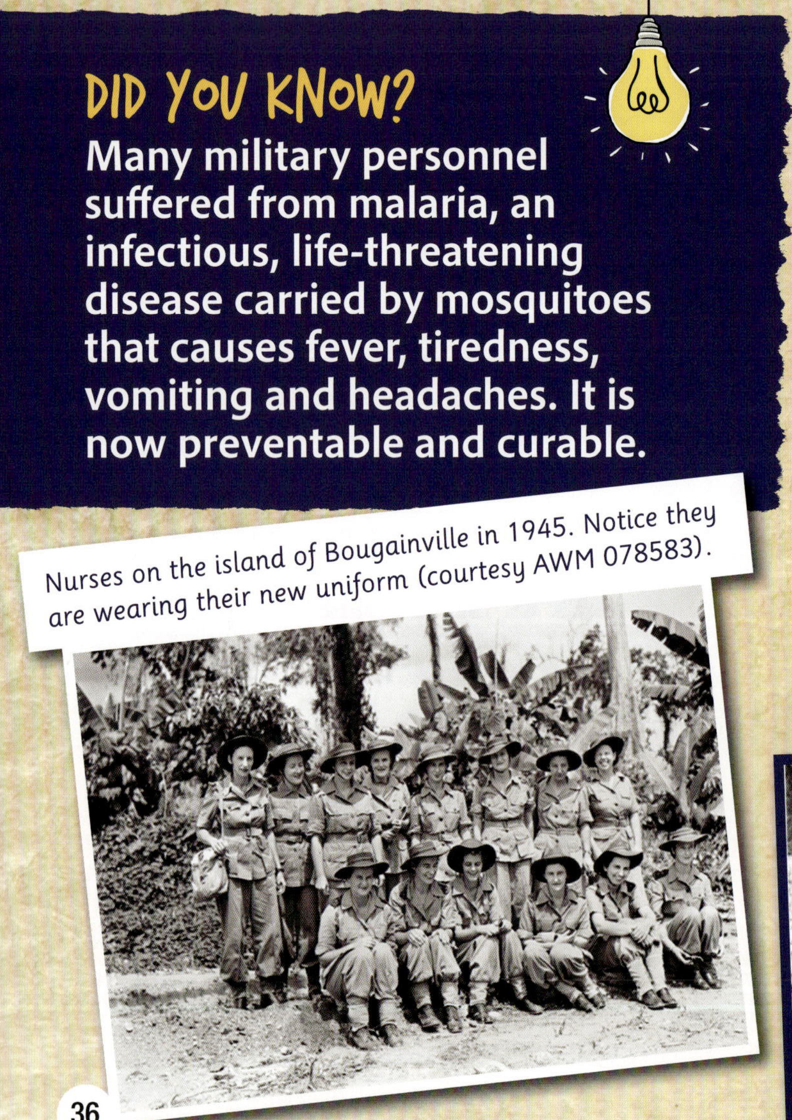

Nurses outside their thatched mess (meals) hut in New Guinea, 1943 (courtesy AWM 053193).

With the war now being fought so close to Australian shores, wounded soldiers were evacuated to Australia for treatment. Many large military hospitals were set up across the country. In the early years of the war, most patients were transported by hospital ship. It was a dangerous journey. Japanese submarines cruised the seas and enemy aircraft patrolled the skies.

Naval Nursing

The Royal Australian Navy Nursing Service (RANNS) was established in 1942. Fifty-six nursing sisters served in the RANNS during World War II, based in Royal Australian Naval hospitals within Australia and in Milne Bay, Papua.

The 2/1st Australian Hospital Ship *Manunda*, despite being damaged in a Japanese bombing raid on Darwin Harbour, was used to evacuate thousands of Australian soldiers from Port Moresby and Milne Bay, Papua, during the war (courtesy State Library Victoria).

DID YOU KNOW?

The AANS uniform was changed to a safari jacket, hat, trousers, gaiters around the ankles, and boots. A change of uniform became necessary to help prevent the nurses being bitten by disease-carrying mosquitoes which were plentiful in the tropics.

What differences do you see between this new uniform and the AANS uniform in World War I?

DID YOU KNOW?

Australian nurse Sister Margaret de Mestre was killed by enemy action in Australia during World War II. She was on board *Manunda* when it was bombed by Japanese aircraft in Darwin Harbour on 19 February 1942. Eleven members of the ship's crew were also killed, and 18 others were seriously wounded.

Chapter 8

PERIL ON THE SEA – THE SINKING OF CENTAUR

On 14 May 1943, the Australian Hospital Ship *Centaur* was on its way from Sydney to New Guinea to pick up wounded Australian soldiers. Among the 332 people on board were the merchant navy crew, the 2/12th Field Ambulance, and the ship's medical staff including 12 AANS nurses. *Centaur* was brightly lit, clearly showing her red crosses. As a hospital ship, she should have been protected from enemy attack by the Geneva Conventions. But at 4.10 am, just north of Brisbane, *Centaur* was torpedoed by a Japanese submarine. She sank in three minutes taking most of the people on board with her. Only 64 people survived including just one nurse, Sister Ellen Savage.

The 2/3rd Australian Hospital Ship *Centaur* (courtesy National Archives of Australia. NAA: B6416, 280).

Sister Ellen Savage

Sister Ellen Savage was asleep in her bunk when *Centaur* was hit. She grabbed her life jacket and ran on deck. The ship was on fire and already sinking, so Ellen jumped into the dark sea. She swam through oil and debris and managed to reach a makeshift raft full of wounded men. Despite being badly injured she tended to the survivors, keeping their spirits up by singing and praying. The survivors spent 35 hours adrift before they were rescued.

Sister Ellen Savage was awarded the George Medal for conspicuous service and high courage.

Sister Ellen Savage (courtesy RAANC archives).

> *Myrle Mostyn and myself were awakened by two terrific explosions and practically thrown out of bed … I registered mentally it was a torpedo explosion … In that instant the ship was in flames.*
>
> Sister Ellen Savage, *Willingly into the Fray*, Catherine McCullagh, page 55

Australians were shocked and appalled by the sinking of the unarmed *Centaur*. The Prime Minister called it 'an entirely inexcusable act'. This terrible war crime was deemed a national tragedy and memorials were erected in many states. The sinking of *Centaur* is still commemorated each year on 14 May by the Centaur Memorial Fund for Nurses in Queensland.

The nurses who perished in the sinking of the *Centaur* (courtesy RAANC archives photo).

FAST FACT

The Leask family lost three sons on *Centaur*, all serving with the 2/12th Field Ambulance.

The *Centaur* Memorial Window at Concord Repatriation General Hospital, Sydney (courtesy Sydney Local Health District).

FAST FACT!

Centaur's final resting place was found in December 2009. She lies off the southern tip of Moreton Island on the Queensland coast. Despite almost 70 years under the sea, her red crosses were still visible.

The commemorative sculpture in Brisbane's Anzac Square Shrine of Memories. It represents *Centaur* and (from left to right), a merchant navy seaman, a medical orderly from the 2/12th Field Ambulance, a medical officer, and the AANS Matron who were on board.

Chapter 9

CAPTURED – AUSTRALIA'S PRISONER OF WAR NURSES

Over 100 AANS nurses were stationed on the Malayan Peninsula (modern-day Malaysia) when the Japanese forces attacked. Despite their reluctance to leave their patients, on 12 February 1942 they were ordered onto the last few ships to leave Singapore before it fell to the Japanese.

Those who were crammed onto the cargo ship *Empire Star* with soldiers and civilian women and children were bombed by Japanese aircraft. Some people were killed and others wounded. The nurses immediately took charge of the wounded, even covering them with their own bodies as the Japanese aircraft attacked again. Though damaged, *Empire Star* eventually reached Australia. Two nurses were recognised for their bravery. Staff Nurse Margaret Anderson was awarded the George Medal and Staff Nurse Vera Torney was made a Member of the Order of the British Empire.

Nurses in the hold of the cargo ship *Empire Star* after fleeing Singapore, February 1942 (courtesy Julie Finucane collection).

None of us wanted to leave, we all wanted to stay and look after our patients, but in the Army one has no choice.

Sister Baldwin-Wiseman, 2/13th AGH, on leaving Singapore, February 1942, *Guns and Brooches*, Jan Bassett, page 139

The last group of 65 AANS nurses to leave Singapore aboard the vessel SS *Vyner Brooke* were not so lucky. The small, slow-moving ship was overcrowded with many women, children and wounded soldiers when Japanese aircraft attacked on 14 February. The nurses helped the civilians and wounded into the lifeboats and then leapt into the sea as the ship went down.

Many people drowned, including 12 nurses. The other nurses and survivors spent hours in the water clinging to wreckage. They eventually reached land in various spots along the coast of Bangka Island off Sumatra, Indonesia, where they were captured by Japanese soldiers.

Nurses from the *Empire Star* arrive safely in Brisbane, 1942 (courtesy John Oxley Library, State Library of Queensland).

In happier times, left to right, Sister Dora Shirley Gardam, Sister Ellen 'Mavis' Hannah and Matron Irene Drummond. Of these three *Vyner Brooke* nurses only Sister Mavis Hannah survived (courtesy RAANC archives).

Sister Vivian Bullwinkle ~ Australian War Heroine

Sister Vivian Bullwinkle was just 26 years old when she survived the sinking of *Vyner Brooke* and washed up on Radji Beach, Bangka Island, with 21 of her fellow nurses. Vivian was the only one of this group of nurses to survive an attack by Japanese troops. Wounded in the side, she hid in the jungle where she came across a badly wounded British soldier. She cared for him for 12 days until they eventually surrendered to the Japanese.

In the prison camp on Bangka Island she was reunited with the other 31 surviving *Vyner Brooke* nurses.

For the rest of her life, Vivian devoted herself to the care and support of nurses. She received many honours and awards including the Royal Red Cross, the Florence Nightingale Medal, Order of Australia Medal, and she was made a Member of the Order of the British Empire.

> *I felt that if my friends were prepared to go and fight for their country, they deserved the best care that we could give them.*
>
> Sister Vivian Bullwinkle, OAM MBE, ABC Documentary *Vivian Bullwinkle An Australian Heroine*

Sister Vivian Bullwinkle at Puckapunyal Army Camp, Victoria, in 1941 (courtesy National Library of Australia, Creator Bruce Howard, cat-vn4227531).

As prisoners of the Japanese, the nurses were held captive along with other British nurses and hundreds of civilian women and children. They cared for these civilians, and one another, with few medicines or equipment. For over three and a half years they endured harsh treatment and were given little food. Many fell ill and eight nurses died of disease. After the war the nurses said it was their strong friendships and support for one another that got them through.

DID YOU KNOW?

The war ended on 15 August 1945 with the surrender of the Japanese, but nurses held captive in Sumatra did not find out it was over until 24 August. They were in a hidden camp and at first the Australian authorities were unable to find them. They were eventually found on 15 September 1945.

FAST FACT!

The nurses had such pride in their AANS uniforms that they saved them and, although tattered and stained, wore them on the day they were freed.

Do you have a uniform you wear with pride?

The nurses were flown to Singapore to recover, then sailed home on the hospital ship *Manunda*, arriving to cheering crowds and masses of flowers.

These heroic women who served and suffered together formed unbreakable bonds. They remained close friends for the rest of their lives, and never forgot their fallen sisters.

When together you face the same hardships and challenges that nursing presents, you form friendships that last a lifetime.

Former British Army nurse, Lieutenant Betty Rumney, has remained friends with the nurses she trained with for over 70 years.

The *Vyner Brooke* nurses arrived home to a warm welcome, October 1945 (courtesy State Library Victoria).

This commemorative coin was released by the Royal Australian Mint in 2017 to mark the 75th anniversary of the sinking of the *Vyner Brooke* (courtesy Royal Australian Mint).

Nurses recovering in hospital after years of starvation in Japanese prison camps (courtesy State Library Victoria).

The Rabaul Nurses

The survivors of the *Vyner Brooke* were not the only Australian nurses to be captured by the Japanese during World War II. A group of six AANS nurses and 11 Australian civilian nurses who were working in Rabaul, New Britain (now part of New Guinea), was captured and held prisoner in Japan for over three years. They were rescued in August 1945.

Four of the AANS nurses captured at Rabaul arrive in Australia, September 1945 (courtesy State Library Victoria).

Chapter 10

THE FLYING ANGELS – BRINGING THEM HOME

The Royal Australian Air Force Nursing Service (RAAFNS) was formed in July 1940. Approximately 600 trained nursing sisters served with the RAAFNS during World War II. At first they were stationed in Royal Australian Air Force (RAAF) hospitals attached to air force bases in Australia, but later they served in New Guinea and the surrounding islands.

In early 1944 the RAAF formed a special unit to evacuate casualties from New Guinea and other Pacific islands by air. The Medical Air Evacuation Transport Unit (MAETU) was a fast and effective way to transport sick and wounded troops to larger base hospitals in Australia for treatment.

Six of the RAAFNS MAETU nursing sisters, dubbed the 'Flying Angels', at their base in Morotai, Indonesia, in 1945 (*Argus* Newspaper Collection of Photographs, courtesy State Library Victoria).

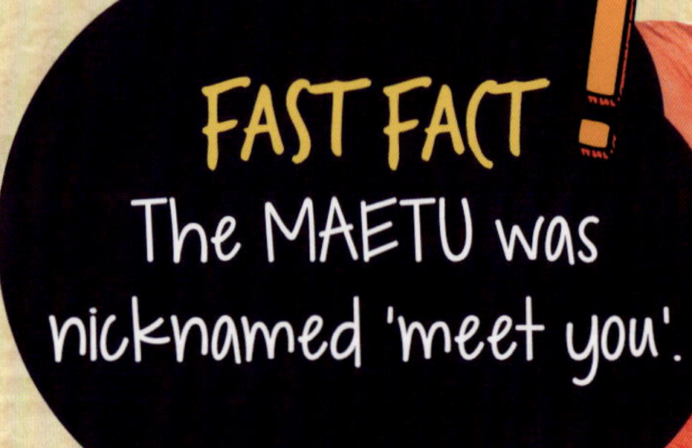

FAST FACT

The MAETU was nicknamed 'meet you'.

The Flying Angels

Called the 'Flying Angels' by their grateful patients, MAETU nurses were specially trained to care for patients 'in flight'. They were also taught jungle and ocean survival skills. MEATU nurses battled airsickness, coped with bumpy landings, and camped rough in the jungle when bad weather made flying impossible. These pioneering women flew into combat zones to retrieve the sick and wounded and saved the lives of thousands of Australian and Allied servicemen.

We had a medical box with drugs and dressings and an oxygen cylinder; a 2 gallon (7.5 litres) thermos of tea … All of us bringing out battle casualties. The boys were all tired, ill and weary.

Sister Joan Loutit, No.2 MAETU, *Caring for the Troops* - Old Treasury Building Website

Why do you think the MAETU nurses were trained in survival techniques?

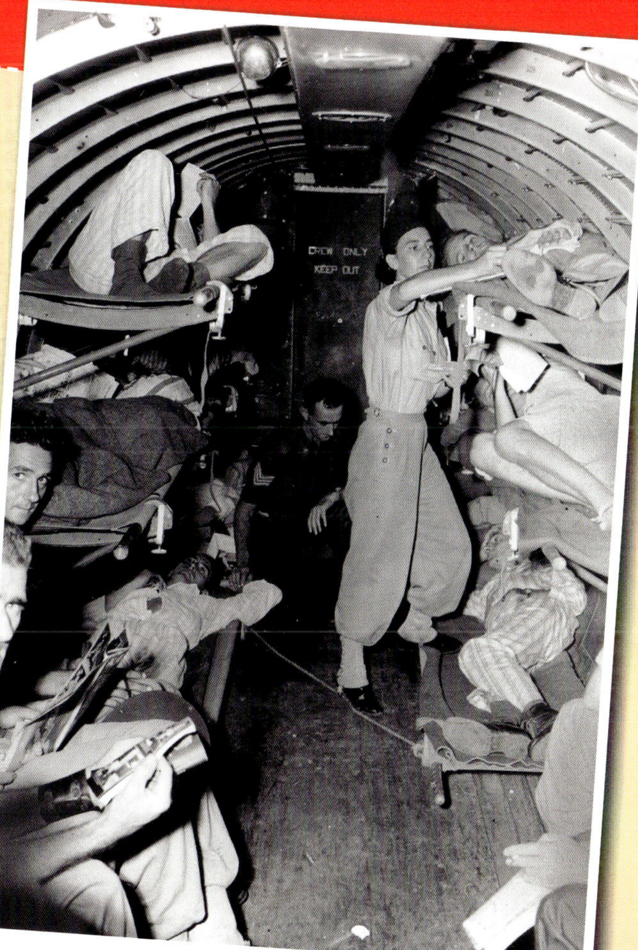

Staff of MAETU check on their patients during a flight from New Guinea, 1944 (*Argus* Newspaper Collection of Photographs, courtesy State Library Victoria).

A 'Flying Angel' catches up on some much-needed sleep between missions (*Argus* Newspaper Collection of Photographs, courtesy State Library Victoria).

FAST FACT!

Seventy-eight Australian nurses died on active service during World War II. Unlike in World War I, most died as a result of enemy action.

The Korean War

Less than five years after World War II ended, Australian troops were once again sent to war. The Korean War (1950–1953) erupted in June 1950 when communist North Korea invaded South Korea. Australia joined the United States and other nations as part of a **United Nations** (UN) force to defend South Korea. Just over 17,000 Australians served in the Korean War. Of these, 340 died and more than 1,200 were wounded. Twenty-nine were held as prisoners of war.

FAST FACT!

The AANS was renamed the Royal Australian Army Nursing Service (RAANS) in 1948. In 1951, the RAANS merged with the Australian Army Medical Women's Service to form the Royal Australian Army Nursing Corps (RAANC).

RAANC nurses sightseeing in Seoul, South Korea, 1953 (courtesy RAANC Archives).

Australian Army and Air Force nurses cared for troops and civilians during the Korean War. Working with Canadian and British nurses, doctors and other medical staff, they treated casualties from Korea who were evacuated by air.

Approximately 30 RAANC nurses also served in the British Commonwealth Communication Zone Medical Unit in Seoul, South Korea. Here they worked in a bombed-out school with no electricity or running water and faced enemy bombing raids almost every night.

Twenty RAAF nurses served in Korea assisting the aeromedical evacuation of the sick and wounded. During the war they cared for over 12,000 patients on flights from Seoul to the RAAF base in Iwakuni, Japan.

DID YOU KNOW?

During the 1950s and 1960s, RAANC nurses were stationed in Malaya (now Malaysia) and in Indonesia to care for Australian and Commonwealth troops fighting against the spread of communism in the region. During what was known as the Malayan Emergency, they treated not only troops, but their families who had accompanied them. They also provided aid to local communities. RAANC nurses remained in Malaysia until 1971.

Medical Breakthrough

The evacuation of wounded troops by helicopter, known as 'medevac', first began during the Korean War. The speed and agility with which helicopters can collect and transport patients to a hospital facility for treatment have saved countless lives during times of war and peace.

The Vietnam War (1962–1973)

In 1966, along with the United States, New Zealand and a number of other countries, Australia sent troops to help the South Vietnamese forces fight the communist North Vietnamese forces which were trying to take over the country. Almost 60,000 Australian Army, Air Force and Navy personnel served in Vietnam until they were withdrawn in 1973. More than 500 of these men died and over 3,000 were wounded.

Along with troops, Australia also sent the 2nd Field Ambulance and later the 8th Field Ambulance, and the 1st Australian Field Hospital (1 AFH). Approximately 150 of Australia's military nurses served in the Vietnam War.

RAANC nurses served in Vietnam from 1967 until 1971. Nurses often worked 12-hour shifts, sometimes longer, treating wounded Australian and allied troops, captured enemy soldiers and injured Vietnamese civilians. Most patients were transported to 1 AFH by medevac helicopter, many arriving within an hour of being wounded which gave them a far better chance of survival.

I always kept my boots and trousers nearby, ready for the arrival of a chopper or a caribou with wounded men who had been evacuated. There were no starched collars at Vung Tau!

Major Nell Espie, Matron, 1 AFH, Vung Tau, South Vietnam, *Willingly into the Fray*, page 214

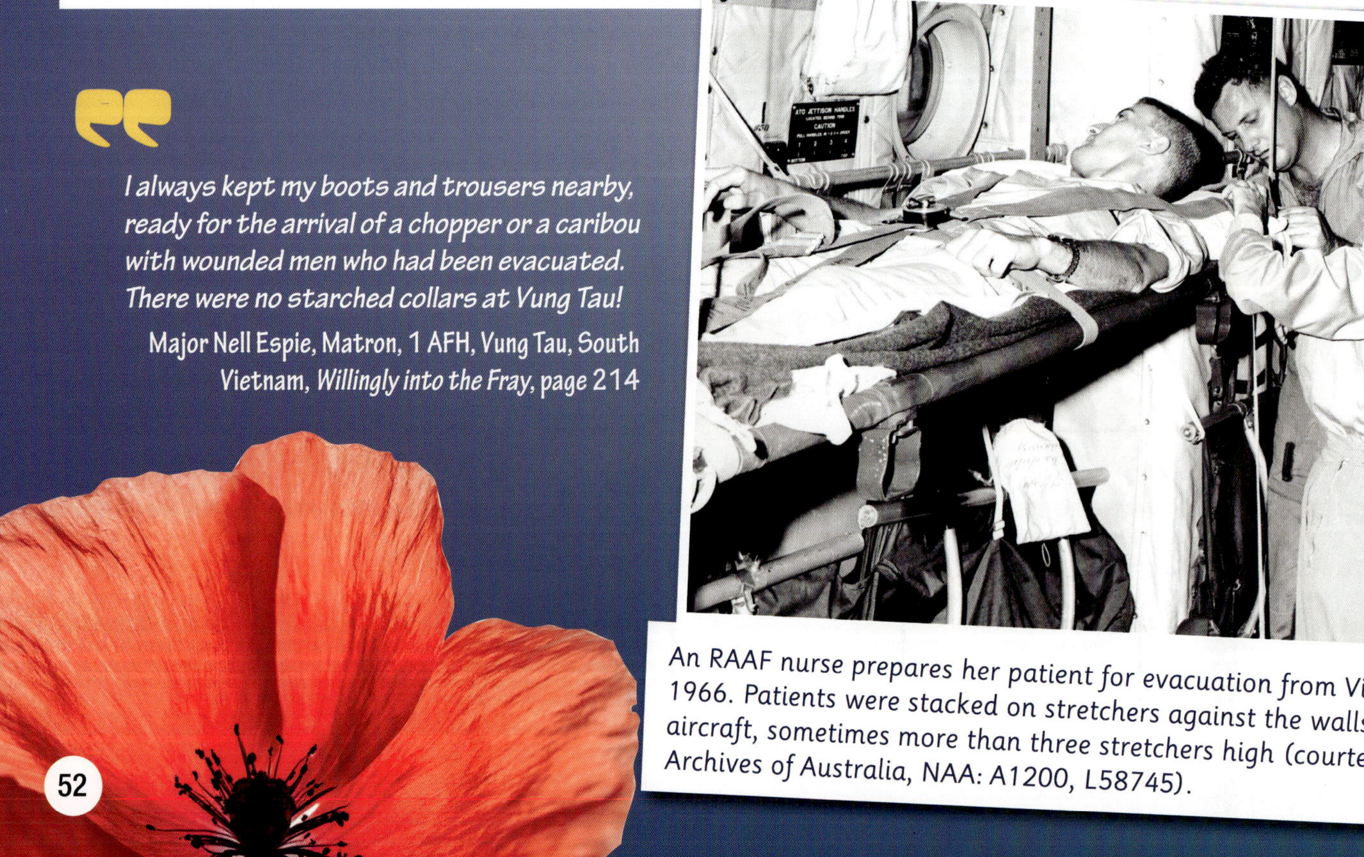

An RAAF nurse prepares her patient for evacuation from Vietnam in 1966. Patients were stacked on stretchers against the walls of the aircraft, sometimes more than three stretchers high (courtesy National Archives of Australia, NAA: A1200, L58745).

One hundred and six nursing officers from the RAAFNS were posted to the RAAF base at Butterworth in Malaysia. These nurses assisted with the treatment and evacuation of the wounded and sick from Vietnam to Malaysia and Australia during the war.

FAST FACT!
Around 200 Australian civilian nurses worked with volunteer medical teams in Vietnam during the war. Many female doctors and other medical personnel also served with volunteer civilian medical aid teams.

We attended all. Allies, civilians and captured enemy. No distinction was made.

Corporal Jeff Myers, who served on medevac helicopters during the Vietnam War.

Women Doctors

In 1970, Major Shirley Coghlan became the first female medical officer to serve officially with the Australian Army in a war zone. She was in charge of the post-operative intensive care unit at 1 AFH. Women anaesthetists, pathologists, radiographers and physiotherapists also served with the Australian Army at 1 AFH in South Vietnam during the war.

Why do you think women doctors were now permitted to serve with the Australian Army in a war zone?

Australian Army field medic Corporal Jeff Myers in front of his US Army medevac helicopter. Notice the red crosses which indicate the helicopter is unarmed and should be safe from enemy fire. Despite the red crosses, hundreds of medevac helicopters were shot down during the war (courtesy Jeff Myers).

Chapter 11

MODERN-DAY MILITARY NURSING

Since the Vietnam War, Australian Defence Force (ADF) nurses have served with medical teams during military and peacekeeping operations and humanitarian aid missions in numerous countries including Cambodia, Somalia, Rwanda, East Timor, Bougainville, Solomon Islands, Iraq, Pakistan, Afghanistan and Indonesia.

In difficult and dangerous circumstances they have provided outstanding nursing care, support, and comfort to troops and civilians of many different nations during times of conflict and crisis.

DID YOU KNOW?

In 1976, the Australian government established the Australian Defence Force (ADF). Nurses from the RAANC, RAAF and RAN became part of the one organisation, the ADF. Qualified nurses in all three services are called nursing officers. Medical teams often include nurses from all three services working together.

FAST FACT!

In 1979 female nursing officers were finally given equal pay with male officers of the same rank.

Did you easily notice their blue hats and red crosses?

Peacekeeping

While involved in United Nations (UN) peacekeeping missions, nurses often work in situations where they are caught between two warring groups. Members of UN forces, including nurses serving with medical teams, wear blue berets, caps or helmets to identify themselves as belonging to a UN peacekeeping force. Light blue was chosen as the colour of their headwear because it is the colour of the UN flag and is easily recognisable.

ADF nurses and doctors at the UN Military Hospital, Dili, East Timor (now Timor-Leste), 2002 (courtesy Captain Paul Luckin RAN).

Private Cruise (military dogs have a name and rank), a valuable army dog, broke a tooth in the line of duty and was in great pain. The ADF medical team stepped in to help. Captain Paul Luckin anaesthetised the dog for an army dentist to fit a temporary tooth, Timor-Leste, 2006 (courtesy Captain Paul Luckin RAN).

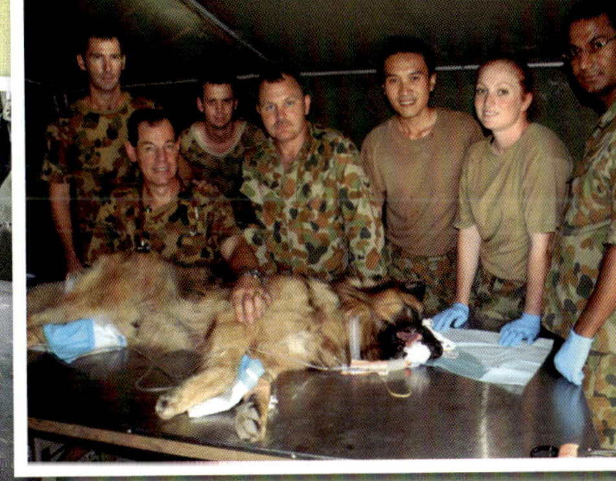

Over 300 ADF medical personnel were sent to Rwanda in 1994 as part of the United Nations Assistance Mission in Rwanda. It was Australia's largest medical deployment since the Vietnam War.

A much happier Private Cruise visits Captain Paul Luckin for his post-operative check-up (courtesy Captain Paul Luckin RAN).

Male Nurses

A shortage of nurses after World War II meant males were allowed to join the nursing profession. The first male nurses to be registered in Victoria in 1946 had been medical orderlies during World War II. In 1972, the first male nurse was permitted to enlist in the RAANC. Currently, around 40% of ADF nurses are male.

FAST FACT

In 1996, Medical Officer Captain Carol Vaughan Evans became the first woman to be awarded a Medal of Gallantry. Carol was the officer in charge of the Australian medical team which treated thousands of casualties from an attack on the Kibeho refugee camp in Rwanda in April 1995.

For two decades Australian troops were involved in an American-led war on terror in Afghanistan. During this time ADF medical teams were deployed to care for Australian, American and other coalition troops, as well as wounded Afghan soldiers and injured civilians — and sometimes injured enemy forces.

What effects do you think serving in a war zone might have on nurses and others in a medical team?

Did you notice that the nurses' theatre hats have Australian flags on them?

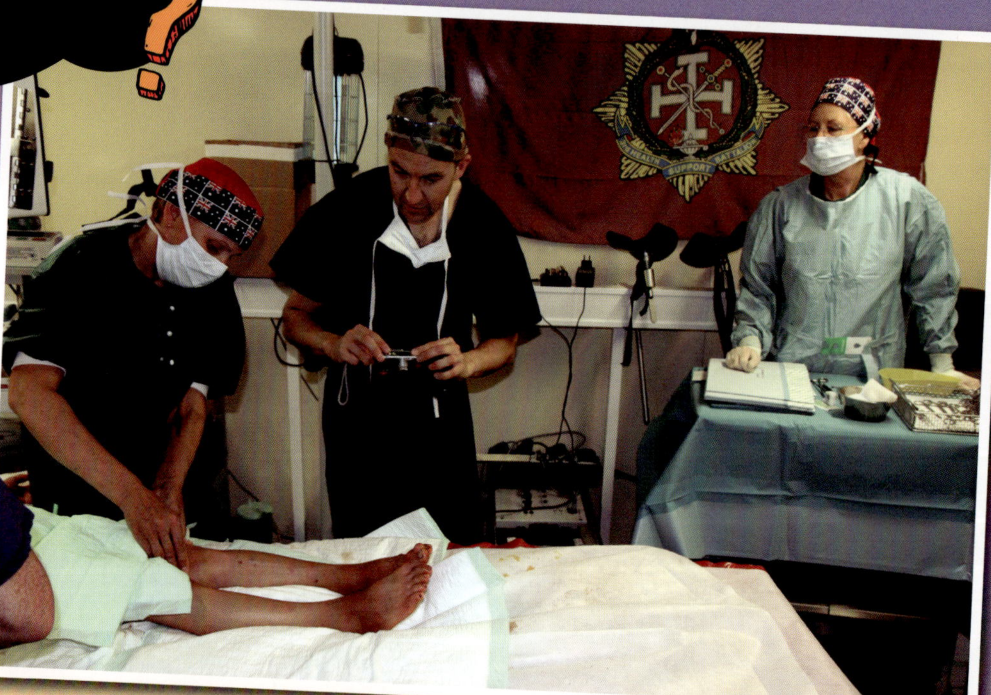

ADF nurses treating a patient and recording injuries at the Coalition Hospital in Afghanistan, 2009 (courtesy Captain Paul Luckin RAN).

Medical Breakthrough

One of the biggest developments in modern medicine came in the early 1900s when it was discovered that human blood consisted of four different types or groups. Human blood is either type O (the most common), A, B or AB (the least common). It is either Rhesus (Rh) factor positive or negative. Being given the wrong type of blood can cause dangerous reactions, even death. During World War II, Australian troops had their blood group recorded on the identity discs they wore around their necks.

Do you know which blood group you, or members of your family, are?

DID YOU KNOW?

Blood was stored in glass bottles until the 1950s. It is now kept in plastic bags which are safer and easier to store and transport. Each bag is called a unit.

A medical team on board HMAS *Adelaide* practise transporting a sick patient to a medevac helicopter, 2015 (courtesy Captain Paul Luckin RAN).

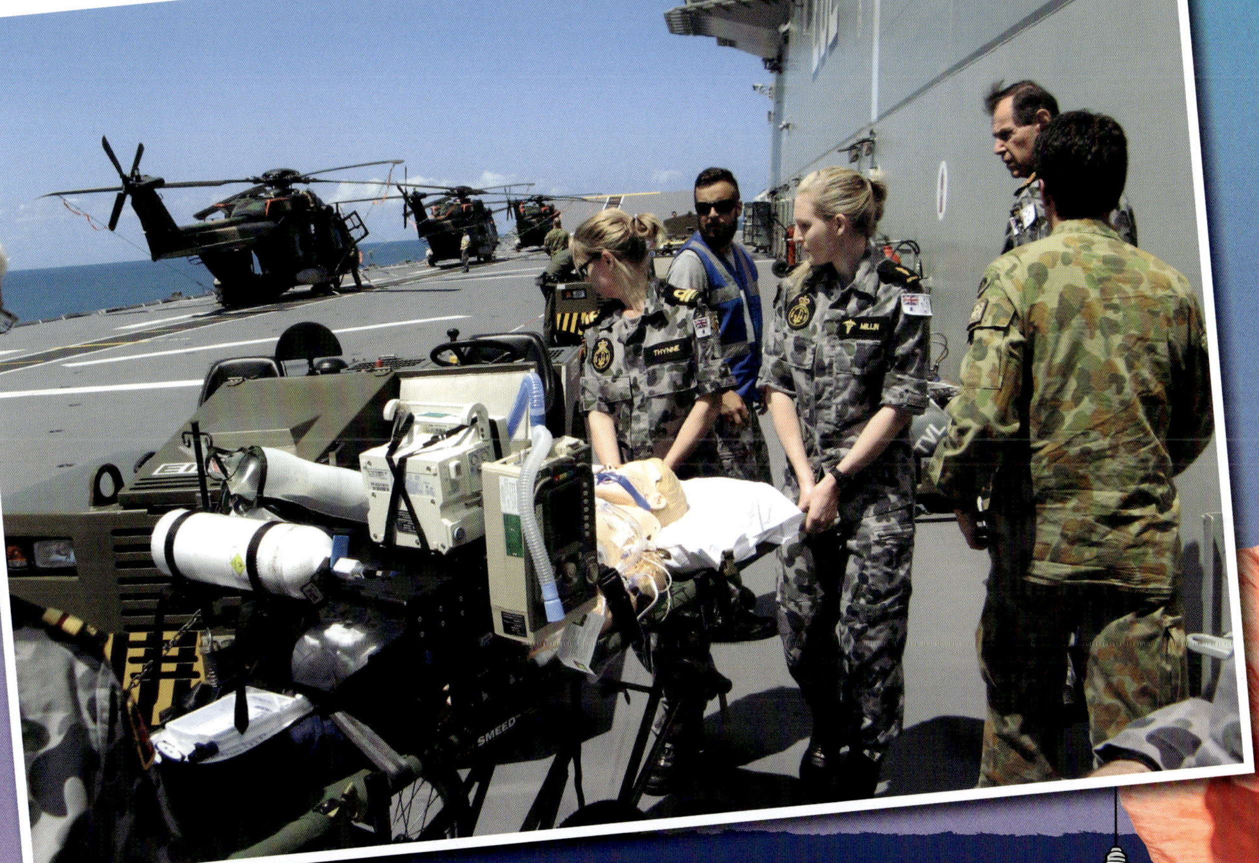

DID YOU KNOW?

While the Royal Australian Navy no longer has designated hospital ships, HMAS *Adelaide* and HMAS *Canberra* have fully equipped hospital facilities, including intensive care units. Helicopters carrying patients land directly on the deck of the ship. There is even a lift to carry patients from the flight deck to the on board hospital.

Tragedy

During Operation Sumatra Assist in 2005, nine members of an ADF medical team were killed when their helicopter crashed on the way to deliver humanitarian aid to the island of Nias, Indonesia. The team included Nursing Officer Flight Lieutenant Lynne Rowbottom.

Exhausted ADF medics sleeping on board an ADF Hercules aircraft bringing victims of the Bali bombings back to Australia during Operation Bali Assist, 2002. This was Australia's largest aeromedical evacuation since the Vietnam War (courtesy Captain Paul Luckin RAN).

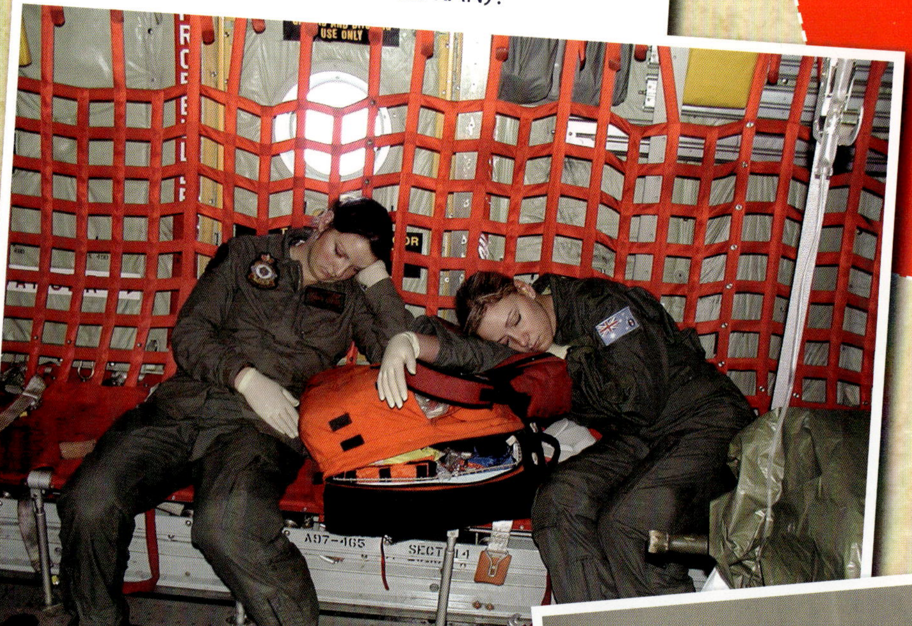

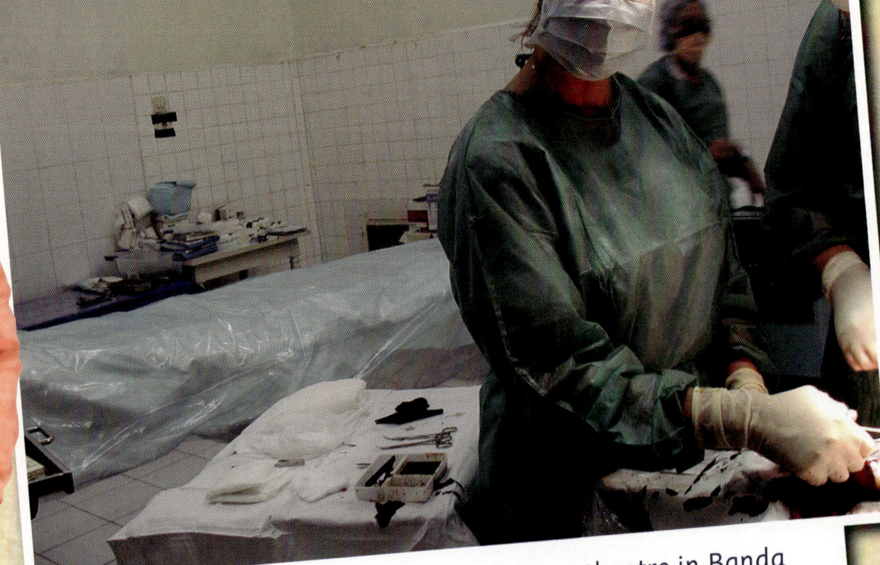

An Australian civilian nurse assists in the operating theatre in Banda Aceh, Sumatra, Indonesia. Following the devastating tsunami on Boxing Day 2004, Australia sent civilian and ADF medical teams to provide much needed humanitarian aid (courtesy Captain Paul Luckin RAN).

ADF nurses also provide aid in Australia during times of natural disaster and emergencies such as floods, cyclones and bushfires. In 2020 they were deployed during the COVID-19 pandemic to help staff COVID testing centres and busy hospitals, and in 2021 they helped to administer and distribute the COVID-19 vaccine.

Australian Army Nursing Officer Lieutenant Samantha Dowdney prepares COVID-19 vaccines at a Vaccination Clinic in Lightning Ridge, New South Wales, September 2021 (courtesy Department of Defence).

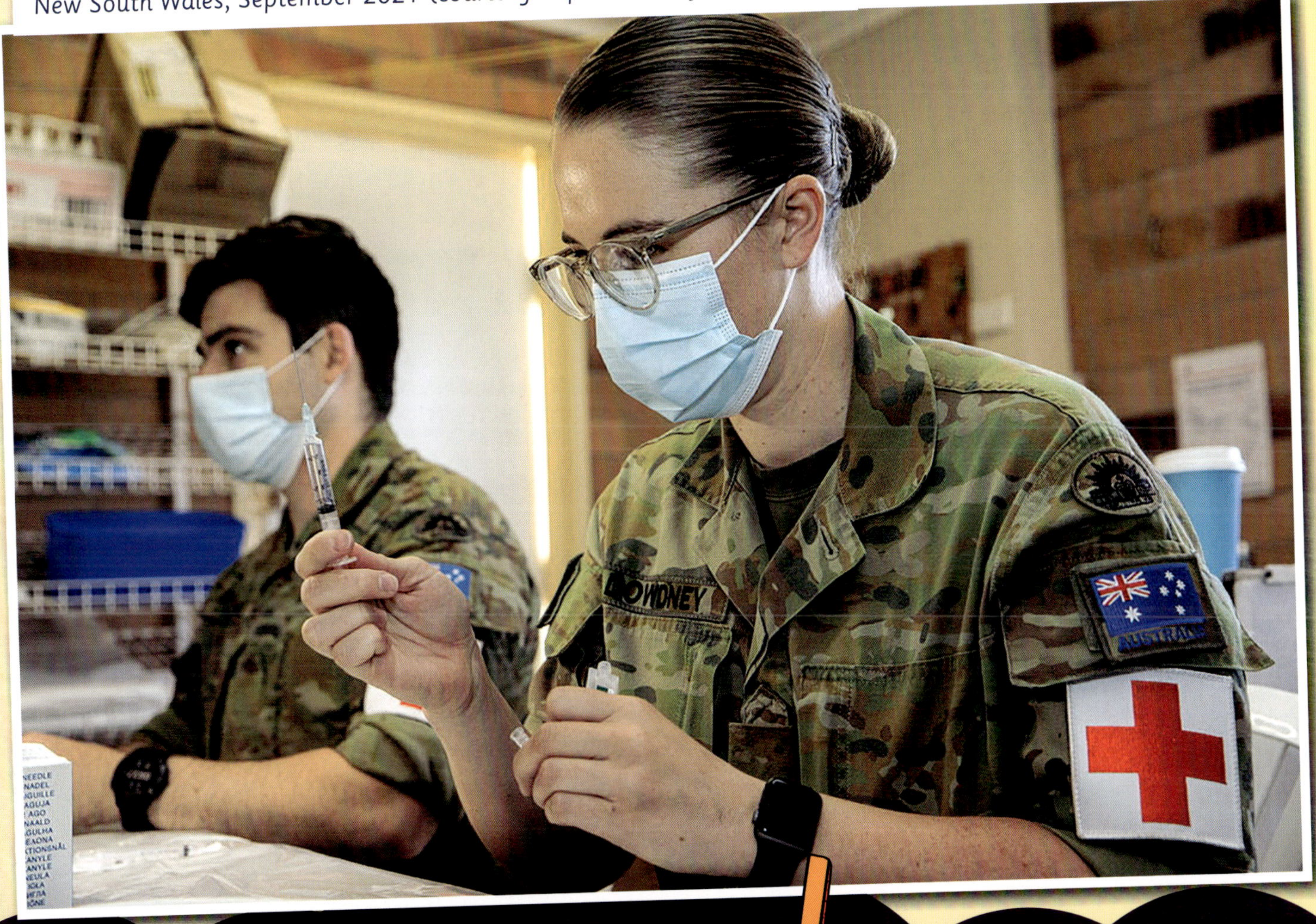

FAST FACT!

Many of today's military nurses are members of the reserve forces who volunteer to serve during times of crisis or natural disasters. More than 800 nurses currently serve in the ADF in either a full-time or reserve capacity.

Chapter 12

MEDALS AND MEMORIALS

Medals are one way in which governments or organisations reward individuals for outstanding service, exceptional bravery or remarkable dedication to duty. They are awarded to military personnel and civilians, during times of war and peace.

Some medals, such as the Florence Nightingale Medal, the Royal Red Cross and the Nursing Service Cross, were created exclusively for nurses. The first three Royal Red Cross Medals were awarded to Australian nurses during the Boer War.

Can you think of other times when people are awarded medals? Does your school give out medals for any special achievements?

This Florence Nightingale Medal belonged to Matron Sadie (Sarah) MacDonald. A former World War I nurse who served in Egypt and France, she was recognised for her lifelong dedication to nursing (courtesy The Queensland Women's Historical Association. Photo by Julie Martin).

The Florence Nightingale Medal

The Florence Nightingale Medal, established in 1912 by the International Committee of the Red Cross, is the highest international award a nurse can achieve. In 1992 male nurses became eligible for the award.

One of Australia's most recent recipients of the Florence Nightingale Medal was nurse Kirsty Boden, who was killed while helping victims of a terrorist attack on London Bridge in 2017.

I'm a nurse. I have to go and help.

Nurse Kirsty Boden said to her friends before she ran to help the wounded on London Bridge.

The Royal Red Cross

In 1883, Queen Victoria, who was a good friend of Florence Nightingale, established the Royal Red Cross medal. It was the first medal of honour exclusively for women. The Royal Red Cross is awarded to military nurses in the British Commonwealth who have shown outstanding devotion or competence, or who have performed an exceptional act of bravery. In 1976, men also became eligible for the award. It was last given to an Australian in 1982. Florence Nightingale was the first recipient.

Matron Ida Greaves, one of Australia's most highly decorated and longest serving nurses of World War I, was presented with this Royal Red Cross medal at Buckingham Palace, London, in July 1915 for her exceptional service in military nursing (courtesy Newcastle Museum).

Nursing Service Cross.

The Nursing Service Cross

The Nursing Service Cross was introduced in 1989 because there was no specific award that recognised Australian nurses. It was awarded to ADF nurses and medics who showed outstanding devotion and skill in the performance of nursing duties during warlike and non-warlike conditions.

During World War I, 388 Australian nurses were awarded medals for their service. They included eight Military Medals, the highest Imperial award given to nurses, 42 Royal Red Crosses and 138 Associated Royal Red Crosses. Twenty-three nurses received medals of recognition and gratitude from foreign governments.

Sister Pearl Corkhill receiving the Military Medal for her courage and devotion during an enemy air raid in WWI (courtesy AWM P01850.006).

Courage Under Fire – The Military Medal

While wartime nursing often required bravery, some nurses displayed exceptional courage under fire. In July 1917, Australian nursing sisters Alice Ross King, Dorothy Carwood, Mary Jane Derrer and Clare Deacon were on duty at No. 2 Australian Casualty Clearing Station (2 ACCS) in Trois Arbres, France, when it was bombed by German aircraft late one night. Despite the threat of further bombing, they worked to rescue their patients from the damaged tents. Sister Rachael Pratt was working at 1 ACCS when it was bombed. Although she was badly wounded, she continued to care for her patients. Rachael was the only Australian nurse wounded by the enemy during World War I. Sisters Alicia Kelly, Eileen King and Pearl Corkhill also stayed to treat and comfort their patients during bombing raids in late July 1917, instead of seeking shelter themselves. These eight brave nurses were awarded the Military Medal for their courage under fire.

?

What do you think their actions during air raids say about the character of these nurses?

Since World War I, many Australian military and civilian nurses have been awarded medals for their devotion to duty, bravery and outstanding care of the sick, wounded and injured.

FAST FACT!

The George Medal, instituted in 1940 by King George VI, was a decoration for acts of gallantry by civilians or military personnel away from the battlefield. Two RAANC nurses were issued this medal during World War II for acts of great courage – Staff Nurse Margaret Anderson, who was aboard *Empire Star* when it was attacked by the Japanese, and Sister Ellen Savage, the lone nurse survivor of AHS *Centaur*.

FAST FACT!

Flight Lieutenant Lynne Rowbottom was posthumously awarded the Indonesian Medal of Valour for her sacrifice and service in Operation Sumatra Assist.

The many medals of Matron Grace Wilson, one of Australia's most decorated nurses (AWM RELAWM31816.001).

Memorials help to remind us of the sacrifice of others. They also provide a place where people can meet to remember and pay tribute to fallen friends, relatives and ancestors. Almost every town and city in Australia has some form of war memorial. The names of 'war nurses' are often listed on these local cenotaphs and on honour rolls in local churches and halls. There are also memorials specifically dedicated to the nurses who served.

Do you have any memorials dedicated to service nurses in your local area?

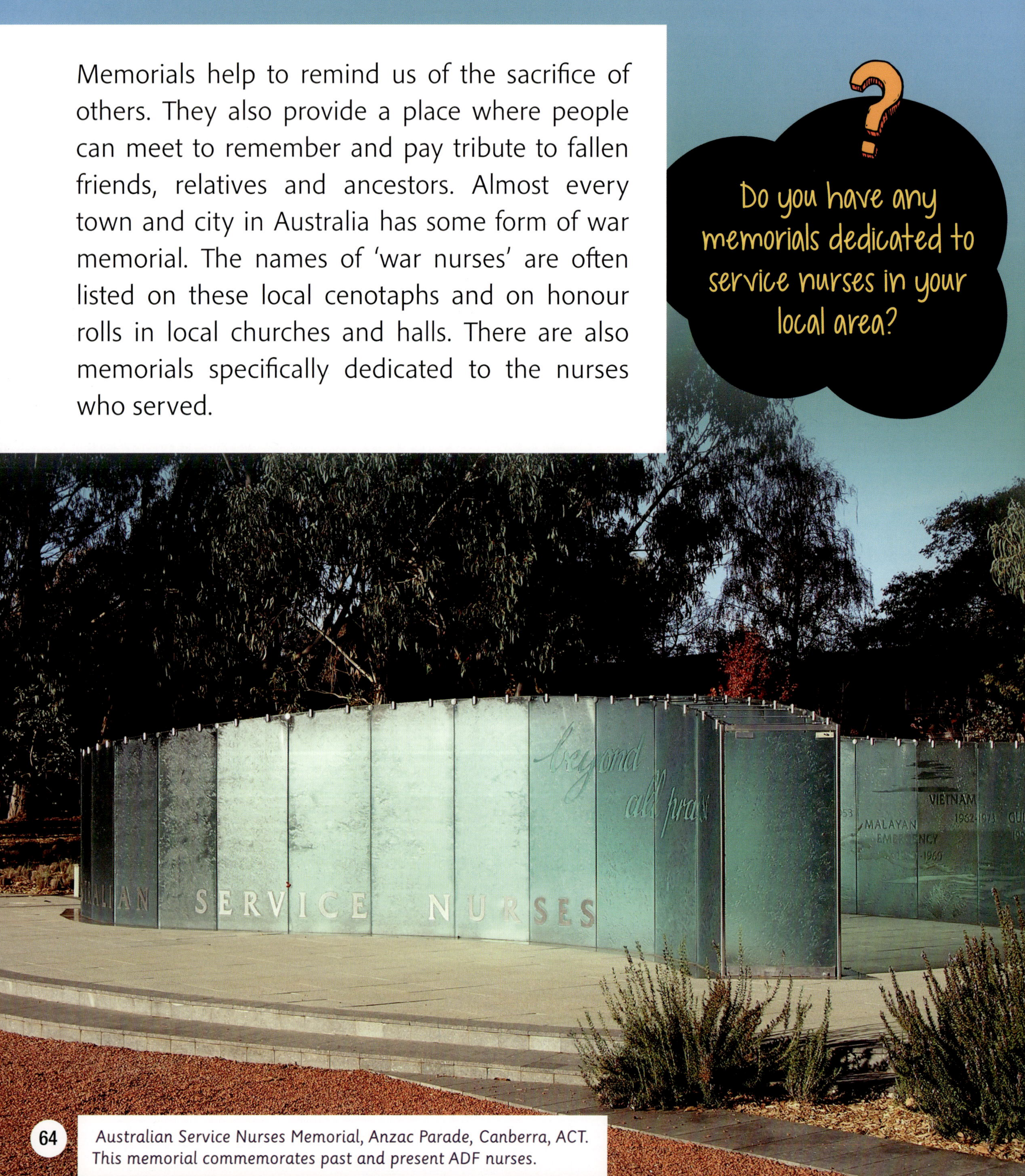

Australian Service Nurses Memorial, Anzac Parade, Canberra, ACT. This memorial commemorates past and present ADF nurses.

Memorials to Australia's nurses take many forms, from statues to stained-glass windows, memorial gates to rose gardens, parks, plaques, buildings and even sundials.

This nurses' memorial poppy was created by Ailsa Bennett from Murrumba Downs, Queensland. The colours represent the AANS nurses' uniform.

FAST FACT!

The World War II nurses' memorial rose garden at Heidelberg Repatriation Hospital is planted with red and white roses, the colours of the nurses' capes and aprons.

The nurses' memorial in Anzac Square, Brisbane.

This triangular coin, released just before International Nurses' Day in 2017, depicts the artwork from the stained-glass window at the Australian War Memorial that is dedicated to nurses (courtesy Royal Australian Mint).

?

Does your school have a special memorial to people who have served in wars?

Commemorative Coins

Numerous coins have been produced over the years by the Royal Australian Mint in recognition of the devotion and sacrifice of Australia's military and civilian nurses.

Chapter 13

THE SACRIFICE OF SERVICE

For over a century Australia's military nurses have been returning from war and peacekeeping missions carrying the emotional and sometimes physical wounds of their service. For people who are committed to caring for others, the immense human suffering they witness cannot easily be forgotten.

RAN Nursing Officer Lieutenant Commander Roneel Chandra on board HMAS *Choules* MRH-90 Maritime Support Helicopter during a medical evacuation, January 2020. Like many ADF Nursing Officers, Lieutenant Commander Chandra has provided medical aid in difficult circumstances and dangerous locations (courtesy Department of Defence).

You don't serve in a war zone without leaving pieces of yourself behind and bringing broken pieces home.

Captain Paul Luckin, RAN

FAST FACT!

International Nurses' Day is held every year on 12 May. The date was chosen because it was Florence Nightingale's birthday.

DID YOU KNOW?

The sacrifice of service is not limited to military nurses. Many Australian civilian nurses work with aid organisations such as the Red Cross. They provide nursing care in locations around the world during times of war and disaster.

From Capes to Scrubs

Over the decades the Australian Army nurses' uniform has changed from thick, grey, floor-length dresses, long, white aprons, veils and capes to camouflage shirts and cargo pants. In the 1990s, civilian nurses were finally given the option to wear trousers. The comfortable tops and drawstring pants many nurses wear today are called 'scrubs'.

RAN Nursing Officer Lieutenant Michelle Price in the Intensive Care Unit on board HMAS *Canberra*, July 2021. The uniform and equipment have changed over the years but the heart of nursing has not (courtesy Department of Defence).

Why do you think the uniform for military and civilian nurses has changed so much over the years?

Year of the Nurse

The year 2020 was chosen as the International Year of the Nurse and Midwife because it was the 200th anniversary of the birth of Florence Nightingale.

There have been many changes within the nursing profession over the past 100 years. But the compassion shown by military and civilian nurses and their dedication to caring for people in need will never change.

Have you ever been treated by a nurse in a hospital, or doctor's surgery or at school?

Australia continues to deploy troops and medical teams wherever they are needed, both in Australia and overseas. With courage, compassion and competence, Australian nurses continue to provide exceptional health care and support for these troops and the communities to which they are sent.

On Anzac Day and Remembrance Day let us commemorate Australian service nurses for the sacrifices they have made, the care they have given, and the lives they have saved. Lest We Forget.

Chapter 14

ACTIVITIES

Make A Red Cross Armband

You Will Need:

- Thin White Card
- Red Card
- Pencil
- Scissors
- Sticky Tape
- Craft Glue

To Make Your Armband

1. From the white card, cut a strip approximately 10 centimetres wide and long enough to go around your upper arm and overlap by two centimetres.
2. Draw a cross on the red card and cut out (see red cross armband on page 24 for guidance.)
3. Glue the red cross onto the centre of the armband.
4. Wrap the armband around your left upper arm and fasten with sticky tape (you may need help with this).

Design A Commemorative Coin

You Will Need:

- White card
- Scissors
- Coloured pencils or markers

To Make Your Coin

1. Cut a circle out of your card to make the coin.
2. Draw a circle on your coin that is a little smaller than the coin itself to create an edge. This edge is where you will write what your coin is commemorating, for example: The Sinking of the SS *Vyner Brooke* 14 February 1942, or World War I Nurses 1914 - 1918, or The Flying Angels RAAF Nurses WWII.
3. Design and colour your coin. Don't forget to write the value of your coin, for example: 50c or $2.

*You don't have to make your coin a circle. The commemorative coin on page 65 is triangular!

Make A Nurses' Poppy To Wear On Anzac Day

You Will Need:

- Red, and white paper
- Scissors
- Grey marker or pencil
- Glue
- Double sided tape or sticky tape

To Make Your Poppy

1. Measure and cut your red paper into a 10cm square.
2. Fold the square in half, then in quarters, then fold it diagonally from one folded edge to the other. Make sure to keep the open edges facing out.
3. Draw a petal shape (or semi-circle) on the wide part of the folded paper, then cut out.
4. Measure and cut the white paper into a 7cm square.
5. Repeat the folding and cutting out as for the red paper.
6. Colour a grey circle in the centre of the white poppy.
7. Fasten the white poppy onto the red poppy with glue or double-sided tape.
8. Stick a piece of double-sided tape onto the back of your poppy. To wear your poppy, peel the backing off the other side of the tape.

GLOSSARY

Advanced Dressing Stations – were staffed by medical officers and orderlies of the Field Ambulance and provided first aid, emergency surgery and treatment before transporting patients on to casualty clearing stations.

Allied/Allies – friendly nations that offer support in times of war.

Boer War – the Boer War (October 1899–May 1902) was fought in southern Africa between Britain and the self-governing states of the South African Republic and the Orange Free State which were controlled by the Boers. The Boers were South Africans who were descendants of Dutch, German or French settlers.

Casualty Clearing Stations – small military hospitals behind the front lines that provided emergency treatment to wounded and sick soldiers before they were moved on to larger hospitals.

Contaminated – polluted or infected.

Convalescent – recovering from an illness or medical treatment.

Civilian – a person who is not a member of the armed forces.

Crimean War – the Crimean War (October 1853–February 1856) was fought between Russia and an alliance made up of France, the Ottoman Empire, the United Kingdom and Sardinia.

Corps – a large group or unit of military personnel who work together. It is pronounced 'core'.

Dressing – a sterile pad or cloth applied to a wound to protect it and promote healing. Bandages were often used to hold dressings in place.

Dysentery – a potentially deadly infectious disease, easily spread by contaminated water, food or utensils, that causes bloody diarrhoea, fever, abdominal cramps and severe dehydration.

Front Line – the area of fighting in a war that is closest to the enemy.

Imperial – relating to an empire.

Injured - victims of an accident or deliberate act in times of peace, or away from the front line during times of war.

Intravenous - giving fluids or medicine via a needle or tubing directly into a vein.

Masseuse/ Masseur - a person who performs massage.

Matron-in-Chief - the highest-ranking nurse in a defence force.

Medic - defence force person trained to deliver emergency medical aid in the field or assist doctors and nurses in a medical facility.

Medical Orderlies - people who assist nursing or medical staff in a hospital.

Morphine - a strong pain-relieving drug.

Patriotism - the feeling of love, devotion and pride in your country.

Physiotherapist - a person qualified to treat injuries, disease or deformity by physical therapies such as massage, heat and exercise.

Pneumonia - an infection in one or both lungs that makes it difficult to breathe.

Posthumously - occurring after death.

Rank - the levels of authority in the military services.

Reserve Forces - trained military personnel who are not on active duty but can be called up in an emergency.

Sanitation - providing clean drinking water and proper disposal of sewage.

Servicemen - men serving in the armed forces.

Smallpox - a contagious viral, often deadly disease, that caused fever and a scarring rash over large areas of the body and face. By 1979 it had been eliminated through vaccination.

Sterilise - to make something completely clean and free from bacteria and other micro-organisms.

Torpedo - an underwater missile fired from a ship or submarine that explodes on impact with its target.

United Nations - an international organisation established after World War II and made up of many nations, that works to promote international peace, security and cooperation.

Wounded - the victims of enemy or friendly fire in times of war.

INDEX

BIBLIOGRAPHY

Bassett, Jan, *Guns and Brooches: Australian Army nursing from the Boer War to the Gulf War*, Oxford University Press, South Melbourne, Victoria, 1992.

Burrows, Deborah, *Nurses of Australia, The Illustrated Story, National Library of Australia*, Canberra, ACT, 2018.

De Vries, *Susanna, Australian Heroines of World War One: Gallipoli, Lemnos and the Western Front*, Pirgos Press, Cutty Sark Studio, Chapel Hill, Queensland, 2013.

Goodman, Rupert, *Queensland Nurses: Boer War to Vietnam, Boolarong Press, Salisbury*, Queensland, 1985.

——, *Hospital Ships*, Boolarong Press, Salisbury, Queensland, 1992.

Harris, Kirsty, *More Than Bombs and Bandages, Australian Army nurses at work in World War I,* Big Sky Publishing, Newport, NSW, 2011.

McCullagh, Catherine, *Willingly into the Fray, One Hundred Years of Australian Army Nursing*, Big Sky Publishing, Newport, NSW, 2010.

Neuhaus, Susan J. and Mascall-Dare, Sharon, *Not for Glory: a centenary of service by medical women to the Australian Army and its Allies*, Boolarong Press, Brisbane, Queensland, 2014.

Richardson, Pat and Skinner, Anne, *"Queenie", Letters from an Australian Army Nurse 1915-1917*, Gumleaf Press, Australia, 2012.

Siers, Robyn, *Devotion, Stories of Australia's wartime nurses, Department of Veterans' Affairs and the Australian War Memoria*l, Canberra, ACT, 2013.

Electronic Resources

Australian War Memorial:
www.awm.gov.au

Department of Veterans' Affairs:
www.anzacportal.dva.gov.au

National Archives of Australia:
www.discoveringanzacs.naa.gov.au

The Centaur Fund for Nurses:
www.centaurnursesfund.org.au

The Australian Nurses Memorial Centre:
www.australiannursesmemorialcentre.org.au

ACKNOWLEDGEMENTS

While researching and writing this book it suddenly dawned on me that the nurses I was writing about would have cared for my grandfather on one of his many admissions to casualty clearing stations or base hospitals during World War I. I realised, that had it not been for the skill and courage of these amazing women, I may not have been here to tell their story. As a former registered nurse, daughter of a former British Army nurse and mother of a current registered nurse, it has been a privilege to write about these remarkable nurses. The devotion and bravery shown by these dedicated women and men deserves our recognition and our eternal gratitude.

I would like to thank Diane Evans from Big Sky Publishing for championing this project from the very start and trusting me with it. My sincere thanks to Allison Paterson who patiently guided me through every step of the writing of this book. Thank you to Big Sky's amazing editors, Catherine McCullagh and Denny Neave, and their talented design team.

Special thanks to Dr Madonna Grehan from the University of Melbourne, Jennie Nicholl and Alaine Baldwin from State Library of Queensland, Joy Wilson from the Museum of Nursing History RBWH, Jenny Steadman from the Queensland Women's Historical Association, Arlene Bennett from the Australian Nurses' Memorial Centre, and Pat Richardson (niece of Sr Queenie Avenell, a WW1 nurse).

I would also like to thank the helpful staff at State Library of South Australia, Wollongong Libraries, the Newcastle Museum, Neredith Elliot from Jimbour

House, and Peta MacFarlane from the Sydney Local Health District. To Ailsa Bennett, thank you for creating a nurses' memorial poppy. I hope that through this book more people will be made aware of it.

My heartfelt thanks and gratitude to Paul Luckin and Jeff Myers for their time, support, advice, and their incredible service.

A special thank you to my wonderful mother for instilling in me a love of nursing, and nursing history.

To my loving family, my sincere thanks and appreciation for your love, support and patience throughout the many hours I spent researching and writing this book.

For our nurses serving now, and those who have gone before, thank you. We are in your debt.

ABOUT THE AUTHOR

Jacqui Halpin is former registered nurse, and daughter of a nurse from the 'Call the Midwife' era. She has a keen interest in nursing history and Australian social history. Jacqui has a Diploma of Professional Children's Writing, and is heavily involved in the children's literature industry in Queensland. She is a founding member of Write Links, where she managed the junior fiction critique group for six years, and is the Brisbane Coordinator for the Queensland branch of the Society of Children's Book Writers and Illustrators.

If you would like to invite Jacqui to speak at your school or festival, contact her at: **www.jacquihalpin.com**